SURFING
Mastering Waves from Basic to Intermediate

MOUNTAINEERS
OUTDOOR EXPERT
series

SURFING
Mastering Waves from Basic to Intermediate

Elliott Almond

THE MOUNTAINEERS BOOKS

THE MOUNTAINEERS BOOKS
is the nonprofit publishing arm of The Mountaineers Club,
an organization founded in 1906 and dedicated to the exploration,
preservation, and enjoyment of outdoor and wilderness areas.

1001 SW Klickitat Way, Suite 201, Seattle, WA 98134

First edition, 2009

Manufactured in Canada

Copy Editor: Heath Silberfeld/enough said
Cover and Book Design: The Mountaineers Books
Layout: Mayumi Thompson
Illustrator: Tracie Griffith Tso
Photographer: All photos by the author unless otherwise noted.

Cover photograph: *Greg Burns surfing/paddling in the aqua blue warm water off the coast of Nagigia, Fiji. Nagigia is one of Fiji's many islands famous for its surfing.* © Corey Rich/Aurora Photos
Back cover photograph: *Robert "Wingnut" Weaver at Pleasure Point surf break in Santa Cruz, California.* © Patrick Tehan

Frontispiece: *The waves can be crowded at popular breaks.*

Library of Congress Cataloging-in-Publication Data
Almond, Elliott.
  Surfing : mastering waves from basic to intermediate / Elliott Almond. —1st ed.
    p. cm.
  Includes bibliographical references and index.
  ISBN-13: 978-1-59485-099-8
  ISBN-10: 1-59485-099-2
  1. Surfing—Handbooks, manuals, etc. I. Title.
  GV840.S8A42 2009
  797.3'2—dc22
              2008052328

This book is dedicated to my father, Hy Almond, who generously shared his love of the outdoors with his family in sometimes surprising ways. As I slumped over my desk, furiously highlighting phrases in a long-forgotten college text one Thanksgiving morning, Dad suggested, "Why don't you go surfing?" Also, to Terry Brian (1952–2008), a real-life Indiana Jones who lived in Seattle and Patagonia, and who helped me navigate difficult sections of life the way he successfully rode through rapids on the Colorado River.

Contents

*Opposite: Surfers walk along the unstable cliffs
above Steamer Lane. They jump from the cliffs
into the sea.*

Acknowledgments

This project would not be possible without the shared adventures and wisdom of the Kenney clan—John, Dan, Chick, and Vicki and her husband, Keith (Grasshopper) Shequin, who often broke into the Elliottmobile to redecorate the dashboard with paper cutouts proclaiming "Inland geeks go home." Caitlyn and Kelly Kenney patiently posed for photos, and they, with mom Kathy and aunt Chris, offered unwavering support. John Shumate doesn't surf, but he never failed to join us in Mexico or down a patch of suburban ice plant. Joe Martinez laughed at my mindless jokes and never stopped encouraging me to stay **stoked**. Bob (Yorba) Zylius was living proof that The Curse does exist: Wherever Bob went, the waves broke somewhere else. Steve Shequin accompanied me and his brother Keith on some early surf trips.

The 38th Street Gang never will be forgotten; it includes Bob Blanchard, Kirk (Buzz) Busbey, Marie Cruz, Dr. Terry (Ted) D'Amico, the Ebels, Blake English, the Fitzgeralds, Chuck Hayward, Terry Johnston, Kirk Kogel, John McGraw, Tommy Olswang, Brian Slater, Scott Smith, and Ed Zintel. At Grant Street in Newport Beach, Andy, Bruce, and Gary Crane made the transition from the beach volleyball court to the sea as smooth as a late-evening glass-off. Santa Cruz surfers Don Carroll and Danny Anderson expanded my appreciation for wetsuits by taking me to frigid waters up the coast. Tim Harvey, a San Francisco surfer/lifeguard/photo artist, provided erudite observations, this author's photo, and invaluable friendship over the course of three decades. Brent Laucher of Santa Cruz and waitress surfing diva Anna Wankel of San Francisco displayed extraordinary kindness.

Some of the world's most famous surfers and industry experts generously opened their lives to me—some in the past, others for the purposes of this book. Thanks to Shannon Aikman, Hobie Alter, Grant (Twig) Baker, Jericho Poppler Barthlow, Tim Bernardy, Duke

Brouwer, the Bronzed Aussies Ian Cairns and Peter Townend, Corky Carroll, Jeff Clark, Sean Collins, Hillary Craven, Mary Lou Drummy, Phil Edwards, Lenny Foster, Ricky Griggs, Jack Haley, Laird Hamilton, Lorrin Harrison, Fred Hemmings, Glenn Henning, Rick Herzog, Maggie and Marissa Hood, Todd Johnson, Bruce Jones, Hunter Joslin, Danny Kwok, Brett Lickle, Josh Loya, Dan Mann, Toby Martin, Greg Miller, Casey Mills, Dr. Andrew Nathanson, Sander Nauenberg, Margo Oberg, Jack O'Neill and Marilyn Trimble, Evan Slater, Rell Sunn, Mark Richardson, Shaun Tomson, Jodi Wilmott, Zack Wormhoudt, and Santa Cruz women warriors Sarah Gerhardt and Sierra and Hailey Partridge. Steve Pezman, publisher of *Surfer's Journal*, shared his wealth of surfing knowledge and has been a nourishing soul for three decades. Surfer/author Matt Warshaw, shaper John Mel, famed surf photographer Aaron Chang, world-class surf school instructors Matt Cole and Ed Guzman, and the ever-gracious Jenny Useldinger offered profound insights. Alexis Pasquariello captured the beautiful image of Useldinger, and Alex Elmore posed for photos. Patrick Tehan, a colleague at the *San Jose Mercury News*, generously collaborated on the color photos and artist Tracie Griffith Tso provided the illustrations.

Ron C. Judd isn't what you'd call the prototypical surfer, but he's one of the best outdoor writers and journalists I've read. His quiet influences can be found throughout this book, as can those from his wife, the writer Meri-Jo Borzilleri, and from Keiko Morris, Jonathan Rabinovitz, and copy editor Heath Lynn Silberfeld. Donna Hewitt, Janet Jones, and Jaime Rupert always were there to listen and encourage. Thanks to The Mountaineers Books über-editors Kate Rogers and Dana Youlin, whose belief in the project brought it to life.

Introduction

It begins simply enough. Grab a board. Rub gummy **wax** on the **deck**. Charge into the roiling surf and ride the waves.

Surfing provides the subtext for athleticism and free-form expression. Some have described it as sport. Others say it's an art form. Surfing actually enlists all these traits, drawing to the ocean the millions who have an unquenchable thirst for adventure and travel.

Yet surfing is not easily defined. To be sure, it's a sport with requisite athletes and tournaments, prizes, and prestige. Equally, it embodies the mystic and poetic in the human spirit that fosters an atypical lifestyle with cultlike vigor.

Athletes and bohemians share a common thread: These denizens drop everything to follow the waves to Hawaii, California, South Africa, Tasmania, even Alaska. They comb the world for waves like the guy with the metal detector rummaging through the sand for loose change.

"The essence of surfing is the connection to me," says Dan Kenney, a longtime California and Hawaii **waterman**. "It's a time when it's just me doing something I feel I'm good at. But I only have to do as good as I want to do. No one is rating me; no one is comparing me; no one is judging me. It is just me doing what feels natural."

He continues: "I love the whole involvement with the ocean and environment, that total commitment to who I am, what I want to be. It is a fulfillment . . . it's just a completion."

Like the waves themselves, surfing hypnotizes the intrepid and turns them into hard-bitten junkies. "What makes the thing so attractive is the rarity of it," says Matt Warshaw, San Francisco author of surfing books and a former professional rider. "On any given day, I'm only on my feet riding for maybe ninety seconds or less. You're not getting much of it. You never feel you've gotten enough of it. You've always got this desire just to keep doing it."

FIRST WAVE

The moment is frozen in time like that ancient iceman Otzi. In the autumnal glow of late October 1971, I found myself paddling into a pine-green wall of water that erupted from a hidden sandbar at Secret Spot, a shore break in San Clemente, California. The defining hour had arrived.

After months of being spilled and tossed by rough **white water**, after session upon session of watching experts in skintight neoprene wetsuits scream across slippery surfaces with the grace of ballerinas, I was about to ride my first wave. My next-door neighbor, the consummate surfer Joey Martinez, offered one word of encouragement: "GO!" he screamed. I went.

The unchecked fury of the ocean boiled underneath as I awkwardly rose as unsure as a drunken man slung over a horse. Then I was up, wobbly right foot forward on the left-breaking roller. The world fell silent. The afternoon westerly winds stalled. Nothing moved but the rolling, green surface of liquid wonder. I was dancing across the ocean's surface at a good clip, but it felt as if movement had slowed to a Sunday drive. The spray from the lip tickled my face as each droplet rushed to greet me.

Then the dreamlike state ended abruptly. The wave began closing faster than I was moving. Surfers below scrambled to the cascading peak. The options were as limited as my abilities. I could continue and let the crashing waterfall knock the board from my feet. I could attempt to straighten the board into the safety of the soup. I chose a third option.

I bailed.

I made a faint attempt at kicking the board **off the lip** before lurching backward, arms flailing, hitting the shallow water hard. I bounced up immediately, wearing a half-moon grin. After I paddled back to the break, Joey paid tribute to the time-honored tradition of dissecting the wave. *My* wave. We celebrated by splashing water on each other.

I didn't catch another one that afternoon. And I didn't care.

I was a member of the tribe.

Steve Pezman has spent much of his adult life reflecting on the meaning of surfing while publishing *Surfer Magazine* and now the elegant *Surfer's Journal.* He divides his thoughts into three categories:

"Athletically, it's as close as man can get to flying, which would seem to be an ultimate sense of free movement and gliding and swooping and defying gravity," Pezman told me.

"It's a dance form. It's interpretive, personal, creative, and very revealing of people because they reflect who they are in the way they move, if they are graceful, or awkward,

Opposite: A surfer stretches the most out of his day at a secluded beach.

or smooth or jerky, intuitive or kind of dense and sealed off to sensory input."

And, "Spiritually, it is a way to connect to nature in that waves are nature's way of transporting energy from one point to another. Because you're dancing, flying and doing all these other components of the experience . . . it may be as whole and revealing to the truth of nature as anything could possibly be."

In the most elementary respect, surfing is categorized into two major forms commonly referred to as **longboarding** and **shortboarding**. The sport began with brave souls challenging the surf with giant, hollowed wooden planks that lacked maneuverability. They were designed to ride the long, slow waves that rolled toward shore in the safe harbors of Polynesia. With the advent of petroleum-based products, surfboard designers began whittling down those monster boards into small, aerodynamic

Riding on top of the wave's lip

A 1960s convertible with a surfboard sticking out the back conjures images of a time when surfing was popularized through surf music and Hollywood movies.

instruments. With myriad variations of design, these new boards allowed surfers to tackle large, tubular waves or race-car-fast **shore breaks**.

Starting thousands of miles from shore, waves are generated by wind or some sort of geological influence. When those **breakers** finally reach close to land they are formed into surfing waves by **reef breaks, beach breaks,** and point breaks. These physical landmarks create waves that crest to the right, left, or sometimes both ways.

The heterogeneity of breaks has propagated mini colonies of devotees who have adopted surfing styles that fit their local waves. Each locale requires a specially designed surfboard calibrated to handle the type of wave distinctive to the break. Although experts could ride one board in multiple conditions, most own a **quiver**, a collection of different styles of boards that

A left-breaking wave at 18th Street in Newport Beach, California

allows them to choose the best one for the break they want to challenge. They do this because boards react differently in big or small, fast or slow, waves.

Beginners, however, only need to worry about the basics once they decide to take the plunge. This book encompasses more than three decades of personal experience to help novices venturing into uncharted waters find their way. Learning to surf doesn't have a singular paint-by-numbers approach. It takes a combination of instruc-

tion, trial and error, experimentation, and following the advice offered in this book, which provides detailed explanations of all the basic skill sets needed to begin. You can learn (or review) proper techniques for paddling, sitting on your board, and eventually standing up and sliding across the smooth, translucent surface of a wave. You can learn how to safely dive underneath oncoming breakers and where to catch a good wave.

This book will guide you to the right kind of board for beginners and will teach you how to use all the necessary equipment, such as **surf leashes, wetsuits,** and choosing a wax for waxing the board. It will provide a basic understanding of oceanography, water safety, and training tips so you are prepared to handle the potential risks. Terms defined in the glossary at the back of the book are boldfaced in the text the first time they are mentioned.

Becoming fluent at surfing, though, involves more than simply jumping into the ocean with a rented surfboard. It's a lifestyle with its own language and unspoken rules. At first it will feel as foreign as the first day at a new school. You will encounter no Talmudic guidelines defining surfing's laws, customs, and mores. You will be introduced to this strange, mystical world through explanations of its rich history, secret customs, and etiquette, as well as an exploration of surfing's unique culture, all of which will lead you into the water confidently. Be prepared to test yourself against nature's elements in new and profound ways.

Mostly, it's time to prepare for the bullet-train ride of your life. Once on board, you're likely never going to stop.

Crouching low near the wave's lip

SOME TERMS YOU'LL HEAR ON THE BEACH

A-frame: A wave that rises up with steep, hollow shoulders and can be ridden right or left. The allusion to an A-frame structure comes from the highest cresting point being in the center of the breaking wave.

aggro: Australian slang meaning "aggressive surfing" or "acting aggressively toward other surfers."

air: "Getting air" can describe doing an aerial, but surfers also "get air" when gathering speed off a bottom turn, hitting the lip of the wave, and flying momentarily before heading back down the wave's shoulder.

alaia: An early version of a surfboard ridden by common and royal Hawaiians before nineteenth-century immigrants wiped out the surfing culture. (The Hawaiian monarchy also had longer olo boards.) Alaia boards usually were made of koa wood and had a round nose and square tail.

aloha shirt: Also known as a "Hawaiian shirt," the fabric borrows the name for the famous island salutation for hello and good-bye. The brightly colored shirts were first made in floral patterns, but modern-day knockoffs cater to other whimsies: surfing, cars, golf—you name it.

artificial reef: Once championed as a way to open new surfing spots to ever-increasing hordes, these underwater structures can simulate such breaking waves as found at breaks with natural rock, sand, or coral reefs. Artificial reefs that have been built to create waves have met with moderate success. They also have been constructed to develop fisheries and protect beaches against erosion from massive swells.

backdoor: Surfers say "He went backdoor" when a surfer takes off late and ducks into the cresting wave. The name also applies to the steep and dangerous right-breaking section of the Banzai Pipeline that is ridden only sporadically.

backwash: The natural phenomenon occurs when the white water hits a steeply graded beach and is pushed back to sea. When the backwash and oncoming waves crash into each other, it creates a new wave, but it isn't a wave conducive to good surfing.

baggies: Swim trunks for guys that fit loose around the legs, once called *jams*.

bail: To bail out or let go of your board in the face of an oncoming wave or during a severe wipeout.

Barney: Surfers have many pejorative colloquialisms for beginners. *Barney* refers to someone who is out of his or her element.

beavertail: A cumbersome wetsuit jacket from the 1970s, with a flap in the back that could be attached to the front when wrapped under the legs. The design was uncomfortable, and many surfers let the flap hang in the back like a tail.

Bells Beach: A famous right-breaking reef break in the state of Victoria, Australia.

Bettys: Slang for surf groupies or young female sunbathers.

Billabong: An Australian surf clothing manufacturer that also sells wetsuits and other surf gear. Unlike other clothiers that have supplied major department stores, Billabong has catered to specialty surf shops. The name is an Aussie word for a stagnant body of water.

blackball: A lifeguard's flag that is yellow with a big black dot in the middle. It signifies that the beach is closed to surfing. Some beaches shared by swimmers and surfers have designated times for surfing because it is unsafe for swimmers to compete with surf riders.

boardies: An Australian expression for baggies or swim trunks.

bomb: A name given to an especially big wave that pops up in a set every so often.

boneyard: The danger zone, or impact zone, of some of the world's hazardous breaks. Also exposed reefs where surfboards go to die. One such famous break can be found at Doheny State Beach in Orange County, California. Boneyards produce a clean wave at low tide but wreak havoc on surfers and their boards when they fall.

Bonzer: One of the first surfboard designs to experiment with multiple fins. The Bonzer was the 1971 creation of Duncan and Malcolm Campbell of Oxnard, California. The bottom of the board also had concave channels by the tail. Though the design ultimately was rejected by the marketplace, the Bonzer helped pave the future of surfboard design.

bowl: A curving section of the wave that rises up quickly because of a shallow reef or sandbar and seemingly bends toward shore. The ocean bottom can cause this type of wave, or section of wave, to break more hard, fast, and hollow than a normal wave. Bowls often are prime tube-riding waves.

brah or **bro:** Pidgin English that refers to a friend. An abbreviation of "brother." Also used commonly as a replacement for "dude" or "Hey, you."

buoy: A floating device anchored to the seafloor to mark a navigational path for ocean traffic or for fishing or meteorological collection data.

charging: Describes those who aggressively ride big waves.

classic: An epic day of surfing.

cleanup set: Often when a swell is rising, a larger wave, or set of waves, breaks beyond the lineup where surfers are situated. Except for the perceptive few who see the cleanup set coming, the majority of riders are caught inside and swept toward the beach. Hence, the name "cleanup" set.

climb and drop: An up-and-down maneuver on a wave's face, something like pulling a zipper back and forth. By quickly descending and ascending a wave, a surfer can gain acceleration.

covered: To get covered, or covered up, means to partially disappear under the curl. This is not considered a full-on tube ride because it occurs in smaller surf that is often not conductive to barrel riding.

cross-step: The time-honored method of walking foot over foot on a longboard.

da kine: A Hawaiian expression that describes something that is special, especially a wave or ride. Also used when you can't think of the word for something: "Pass me *da kine*."

Snug wetsuits and specially designed boards are part of the equipment needed to surf.

dawn patrol: Those hearty surfers who hit the beach at sunrise when the waves often are glassy and the lineup void of crowds—unless a big swell is running.

deck patch: To avoid dents, shapers reinforce the deck with extra fiberglass to strengthen the spots where surfers have placed their knees, hands, and feet.

dig an edge: Also known as "dig a rail." This happens when the rail catches on the water, abruptly slowing or stopping the ride. Most likely to occur in choppy wave conditions.

down-the-line: The section, or shoulder, in which a surfer is headed. Surfers sometimes will look "down the line" to determine what kind of maneuvers they will complete before their first bottom turn.

drop-knee turn: A longboard maneuver in which the surfer bends the back knee to reposition the board.

dude: A generic term for "guy."

dumping: Big, hollow waves that fold over and break hard.

eating it: A way to describe a bad wipeout.

The Endless Summer: Bruce Brown's 1966 classic surfing film, which encapsulated the spirit and adventure of the sport by following two Californians—Robert August and Mike Hynson—around the world looking for the perfect wave.

Fin Control System (FCS): One of the big improvements in surfboard designs. Fins once were glassed into the bottom rear of the board. Then came a removable system with a fin box in which the skegs were screwed into a slit on the bottom of the board. FCS uses plugs placed in the board to hold each fin.

floater: A dramatic maneuver in which the surfer "floats" over the top of a breaking wave by sliding across the foam or a curling lip, then dropping back into the face.

fullsuit: A one-piece rubber wetsuit for the entire body, except the head, feet, and hands. Fullsuits come in a variety of thicknesses but the most popular are combinations of 3 and 2 millimeters or 4 and 3 millimeters of neoprene.

glasser: A person, often a shaper, who laminates a shaped foam blank with fiberglass and resin.

glass-off: Describes when the onshore winds die, usually in the late afternoon or early evening, and the waves become smooth or glassy.

gnarly: Slang for big, intense waves that often are the most dangerous places to surf.

going off: Describes a big swell that hits the coast. "It's going off today."

green room: An affectionate name for the concave barrel known as the "tube."

groin: A structure built to stop or slow beach erosion. Often creates sand buildup at the tip that makes good waves. May be used interchangeably with "jetty."

grommet: A neophyte surfer. Often shortened to "grom." Its precursor is "gremmie," a pejorative term from the 1950s and 1960s to describe beginners or wannabes.

Haole: The name Hawaiians gave Caucasian missionaries who populated the islands in the nineteenth century. It has become a mostly derogatory word referring to white people in Hawaii.

hotdogging: Part of surfing slang from the 1950s and 1960s. Refers to trick surfing on small waves, or showing off.

howzit: Hawaiian slang meaning "How is it going?"

inconsistent: Describes a swell that produces waves infrequently. The waves in a set are measured by their duration. When it is inconsistent, it is difficult to predict the frequency of the sets.

insane: Can refer to a great wave or a great ride or, conversely, a scary situation.

in the soup: Refers to riding the broken wave in the foam or white water.

Jeffreys Bay: One of the famous South African surf breaks because of its long lines of right-breaking waves. It was made famous in the movie *The Endless Summer.* Located near Port Elizabeth. Also known as J Bay. Like almost all major breaks, surfers have given Jeffreys Bay's different sections affectionate names: Boneyards, the Point, Tubes, Supertubes, and Magnatubes.

kelp: Marine plant life (also known as seaweed) that thrives on the Pacific Coast of the United States, especially around the beaches of Santa Cruz, California. Kelp forests are characterized by the odd-looking bulbs that float on the surface. Kelp can help reduce surface chop and keep the waves glassy, but it's also a nuisance to surfers when it's growing in the lineup. It can be difficult to paddle through, and sometimes the board is stalled when plowing through the slippery stuff.

kick: Another way to describe the rocker, or concave shape, of a board.

kick out: Also known as a "pullout." Refers to the final move of riding a wave. It occurs when a surfer "kicks" the board over the fading wave and paddles back to the lineup.

kneeboarding: A once-popular (early 1970s) form of surfing. Surfers rode short, egg-shaped boards on their knees and were famous for their tube rides.

knee paddling: Usually done on a longboard, some surfers will balance on their knees to paddle out instead of lying on the stomach. Surfers sometimes knee paddle to take a break from the prone position.

kook: A derogatory term for an outsider or beginning surfer.

layback: A trick move during a cutback in which the surfer bends his or her upper torso into the wave's face.

A steep takeoff is part of the thrill.

left: A wave that breaks to the surfer's left when paddling down the face. The preferred wave for goofy-foot surfers.

locals: Regulars at surf spots. They can earn their entrance by surfing one particular break all the time or simply by living near the break. Crowded conditions over the past thirty years have led to the term *localism,* which refers to locals who band together to discourage outsiders from surfing their favorite spot. This has led to some ugly, violent beach incidents.

locked in: Another way to describe tube riding. It means to be "locked inside" the tube.

logger: A surfer who rides a beat-up, old-fashioned longboard known as a log.

lull: The period during a swell that is calm, without waves. It can occur during a swell, but it also refers to when no swells are to be found.

mushy: Describes slow-breaking, unformed waves that are the opposite of tapering shoulders or hollow cylinders. The soft breakers, though, are ideal for beginners.

mysto spot: A "mystery" surf break. A secret spot that is known by few or is not easily accessible. Also, breaks that produce waves under rare perfect conditions.

neoprene: The synthetic-rubber material from which wetsuits are made.

off the top: Describes a number of surfing maneuvers, such as hitting the lip, roller coasters, and any other trick in which the surfer has attacked the wave's crown and is preparing his or her descent.

old school: Surfers who cling to past styles of boards, clothes, and even the way they ride the waves.

ollie: Borrowed from skateboarding, a style of aerial performed above the wave.

outside: The zone outside the break where surfers wait for waves, or the *lineup*. Also used to let others know a big set is approaching beyond the lineup.

pinstripe: A thin, decorative stripe down the center of a board.

pit: The trough, or bottom section, of a barrel, where the most critical of bottom turns must be completed and where a surfer must navigate in order to set his or her line through the tube.

pitched: To be thrown off the wave's crest or, in general, from your board.

planer: An electric power tool that became the most important instrument for the surfboard shaper in pruning foam blanks, even though most handmade boards are now trimmed by computer-assisted laser cutters.

polystyrene: A sturdy plastic Styrofoam used to make surfboard blanks (and packaging for electronic equipment). Used with epoxy resins instead of the industry-standard resins once employed in surfboard manufacturing.

polyurethane: A light, durable plastic foam material. Available as molded forms that are sanded and cut into specific designs, then coated in layers of fiberglass with polyester resins hardened by chemical catalysts. For more than a half century, this material was used to make virtually all surfboards.

popout: A name, often used with derision, for boards produced on an assembly line.

poser: A person who can't surf but acts as if she or he is part of the surfing scene.

pullout: The process of exiting a wave that is fading or closing out; also, kickout.

pummeled: Describes a bad wipeout or loss of the battle against the pounding surf when paddling to the lineup.

pumping: Describes great surf conditions. When a swell is up, surfers say, "The waves are pumping." It also is an up-and-down maneuver employed to gain speed on the wave.

Quiksilver: The surf-wear company began selling board shorts in 1973 and has become an industry giant, selling to major department store chains as well as boutiques. In 1991 Quiksilver began marketing Roxy, a popular line of women's beach fashions.

rad: Short for "radical." It can mean a difficult maneuver, section of wave, or general surfing conditions.

ragdolled: Describes being held underwater, usually in the impact zone, and being tossed and turned as if in a washing machine.

rail grab: A way to gain stability while crouching in the back-side position during a tube ride.

red tide: A phenomenon occurring near shore that appears to give the sea a rusty, murky hue. It is the result of an algae bloom, but the exact cause for the coloration is unclear.

reef rash: Describes the cuts suffered when falling onto a rock or coral reef. Usually occurs at tropical, shallow-water breaks.

resin: A liquid chemical that is smeared over fiberglass to give a surfboard a protective shell, or seal. Resin hardens when mixed with a chemical catalyst. Surfboard makers generally employ three types of resin to finish a board: a laminating coat, a hot coat, and a gloss coat.

right: A wave that breaks to the surfer's right when paddling down the face.

righteous: Describes excellent wave or surfing conditions.

Rip Curl: A famous wetsuit manufacturer, based in Australia, that later produced clothes and surfboards.

ripping: Describes supreme moves on a wave. Synonymous with shredding or getting rad.

rogue wave: A massive, unsuspected wave that can rise up in the middle of the ocean and is not for surfing. The term often has been borrowed to describe a sudden wave that breaks beyond the lineup and is generally known as a "bomb."

roller coaster: A maneuver in which a surfer angles off the lip almost as if he or she is balancing on a beam like a gymnast. The second part of the trick is to roll down to the bottom.

rubber arms: Describes what your arms feel like after intense paddling. Most beginners will have rubber arms after every session as they develop shoulder and arm muscles. Experts also experience the sensation after a particularly long surfing session or dramatic paddle.

Santa Ana winds: The name given to hot, dry, easterly winds that hit southern California in fall and winter. They form from a high-pressure buildup over the Great Basin region west of the Rockies. These offshore winds are infamous for fueling wildfires, but the feathery waves they create make for heavenly autumn surfing.

scattered peaks: A surf condition in which waves break apart into different peaks or lines with a clear separation between ridable shoulders. This is usually caused by two swells from different directions or periods overlapping the same break.

A small barrel, beach-break wave at 18th Street in Newport Beach, California

shoot the pier: At surfing spots where piers are prominent physical landmarks, daredevil surfers have taken to riding waves between the pilings to cut through to the other side. Some municipalities have passed ordinances making the practice illegal.

short john: A wetsuit that covers the torso and legs to the knees.

shred: Equal to ripping on a wave, to carving radical lines up and down the face.

sick: Refers to a radical or impressive trick. Originated in the X Games generation and came to vogue with aerial surfers.

side-slip: A maneuver in which the fin or fins are released from gripping the water, thus allowing the board to slip down the wave's face. Without any fins being engaged, the surfer has little control. A side-slip usually is performed in small surf.

slash: A quick, jerky turn off the crown that often leaves a tail spray in its wake.

sleeper set: A sudden set of waves breaking beyond the lineup that catches surfers off guard. It is the same as a cleanup set.

sloppy: Describes disorganized, choppy waves that are affected by surface wind or tidal variations.

snake: A surfer who purposefully drops in on someone who has priority to the wave, an act also known as "shoulder hopping." This behavior is a breach of good surfing conduct.

snapback: A quick, short cutback into the power of the wave. Often used in a steep part of the wave when the quick maneuver will keep the surfer in the "power pocket" of the wave. Also used when the wave is too fast for the surfer to have a chance to do a full cutback because the wave would pass by the surfer.

spit: The powerful spray that shoots out at the end of a particularly hollow wave. When air is compressed in the tube, it is flushed out the front with a misty blast. The effects of spitting usually can be seen only on big, tubular waves such as the Pipeline and Tahiti's Teahupoo.

spit out: Occurs when a surfer, inside a tube, is shot out with compressed air and is followed by a trail of spray.

sponger: A caustic description of bodyboarders, in reference to the spongelike boards they ride.

Stinger: A surfboard design credited to Hawaiian Ben Aipa in the early 1970s. The Stinger is characterized by a sudden and dramatic indentation of the rails at the bottom third of the board with a single-fin swallowtail. This board supposedly had more speed because of the narrow tail but also preserved its high-performance capabilities because of the wider body six inches above the tail.

storm surf: Describes big waves with poor conditions, such as strong winds and otherwise stormy conditions, making the surf less desirable.

super late: When a surfer takes off behind the peak or just as it is folding over.

Surfrider Foundation: An environmentally conscious group based in San Clemente, California, that works to protect the ocean.

surf's up: A term from the 1960s meaning that a strong swell is running.

switch foot: A surfer who can ride regular or goofy foot, always facing the wave.

tailslide: A turning maneuver distinguished by the tail end of the board sliding sideways across the wave.

tourist: A word that infers local surfers' contempt for outsiders or beginners.

trimming: The act of angling across the wave's face with supreme speed to keep the board projecting forward.

tsunami: Although often incorrectly referred to as tidal waves, tsunamis are created by an underwater disturbance such as an earthquake or some other major activity. These waves move through deep water at incredible speed and can create fierce waves of thirty-five feet, destroying everything in their wake.

Twinzer: A four-fin surfboard design introduced in 1988 by Will Jobson of Huntington Beach, California, that was meant to greatly improve on the twin fins of a decade earlier. The Twinzer had a narrower tail than the boxy twin fins, giving it speed without loss of maneuverability.

undertow: Often confused with a rip current because an undertow is formed by the same general principle. The powerful flow of water that heads to the sea after a wave has reached the shore.

victory at sea: Describes disorganized, choppy surf filled with whitecaps. The phrase originated from a 1960s television show, *Victory at Sea*.

waterlogged: Describes a dinged-up board whose foam core has become soaked by leakage.

wavepool: A machine-generated wave found in a swimming pool, making surfing available in desert and other resorts and waterparks hundreds of miles from the ocean.

wired: To master a board or surf break. A similar expression is "dialed," as in having a board "dialed in."

woody: A wood-paneled Ford station wagon manufactured in the 1930s and 1940s. Surfers stuck their boards out the back as they headed to the beach—and some still do.

worked: Describes getting wiped out and thrown about while being held under by a wave.

A NOTE ABOUT SAFETY

Safety is an important concern in all outdoor activities. No book can alert you to every hazard or anticipate the limitations of every reader. The descriptions of techniques and procedures in this book are intended to provide general information. This is not a complete text on surfing technique. Nothing substitutes for formal instruction, routine practice, and plenty of experience. When you follow any of the procedures described here, you assume responsibility for your own safety. Use this book as a general guide to further information. Under normal conditions, water conditions, weather, terrain, your capabilities, and other factors all require attention and consideration. Keeping informed on current conditions and exercising common sense are the keys to a safe, enjoyable outing.

The Mountaineers Books

CHAPTER 1

It's time to hit the surf.

Unlocking the World of Surfing

On June 14, 1925, surfing legend Duke Kahanamoku joined friends in Corona del Mar, California, for a Sunday picnic. The group, which included silent film stars down from Hollywood, lounged on the soft sands near Newport Harbor until a woman's screams interrupted them. Just past the harbor mouth, a charter fishing boat, the *Thelma,* had capsized in **heavy** surf with twenty-nine aboard.

Kahanamoku immediately paddled his 114-pound redwood surfboard through the giant breakers toward panic-stricken victims. He reached one, pulled him on his surfboard, and paddled safely to shore. Kahanamoku repeated the effort over and over. Of the twelve people saved that day, eight were rescued by the Duke.

At the time, Kahanamoku already was a famous Olympic swimming champion and the father of modern-day surfing. The Duke, as he was known in his native Hawaii, helped retrace the sport's Polynesian roots by honoring ancient traditions that he shared with the rest of the world. He and his Honolulu beach boys are the connective tissue that has made surfing much more than riding a **wave**. Kahanamoku embodied the true spirit of a waterman/ waterwoman, enjoying a surfing lifestyle until he died in 1968. The lifestyle encompasses paddling, free diving, and ocean swimming. The rescue involving the *Thelma* underscored the importance of physical fitness and knowledge of water-safety skills that remain relevant today.

A BRIEF HISTORY OF THE SPORT

It's thought that surfing began sometime around AD 1000, with indigenous peoples in Polynesia riding carved-out koa trees. Scholars suggest it spread as Pacific Islanders migrated across the ocean from Indonesia. They believe the sport was most pronounced in Tahiti and Hawaii, where some beaches were reserved for royalty who rode especially long wooden boards. It often is referred to as "The Sport of Kings" because Hawaiian chiefs used surfing exploits to assert their position in society. Nineteenth-century scholars unearthed evidence of surfing's importance in Polynesia by translating numerous indigenous songs and chants devoted to wave riding.

Unfortunately, we have no official documentation of the sport's primitive days because Polynesians didn't have a written language. It wasn't until Captain James Cook's explorations of the Pacific in 1778 that the world learned of surfing via the first-known written observations of it, which came from James King, one of Cook's lieutenants. King described Hawaiians' surfing exploits in a journal he kept for his captain, who was killed in 1779 near the Big Island of Hawaii. Writing in the ship's log, King noted that surfing was

done for pleasure, as it is today. It seemed that surfing was interwoven into the fabric of Polynesian society and involved courtship rituals and religious festivals.

Cook's discoveries proved disastrous for surfing. As the first white man to visit Hawaii and Tahiti, he opened the exotic archipelagos to Europeans. It wasn't long before traders, explorers, and missionaries populated the islands, spelling the demise of surfing and other ancient Polynesian practices. For better or worse, the customs and mores of native people were dramatically altered by the influx of new blood, foremost by the spread of deadly diseases. Surfing further suffered in the early 1800s when Calvinist missionaries couldn't grasp the concept of riding waves being productive.

Once an integral part of island life, surfing became a fringe activity practiced by those who refused to be domesticated. Despite its diminished status, the sport continued to intrigue some westerners. In

1872, author Mark Twain described surfing in his book *Roughing It.* He wrote, "Each heathen would paddle three or four hundred yards out to sea (taking a short board with him), then face the shore and wait for a particularly prodigious billow to come along." Twain wrote that he tried, without success, to emulate the Islanders.

SURFING'S REVIVAL

Surfing wouldn't enjoy a rebirth until the turn of the nineteenth century when another famous American author would play a role in helping shape a modern, more adventurous image of the sport.

In 1907 Jack London vividly described surfing at **Waikiki,** Oahu, for popular magazines. At the time Kahanamoku and his buddies enjoyed the rollers that broke in the foreground of the famous Diamond Head peak. With Hawaii transforming into a tourist locale, surfing regained its stature. London's accounts romanticized the daring of one George Freeth, the original bohemian surfer from Honolulu. Freeth, who was a contemporary of Kahanamoku, seemed more interested in capitalizing on surfing's exotic image than the Duke did. Freeth has been credited with exporting the sport to the mainland United States by bringing a board to California in 1907.

Historians have documented Hawaiians surfing in Santa Cruz in the 1880s but Freeth's wave-riding demonstrations along the California coast did more than anything

Opposite: Artifacts of surfing legend Duke Kahanamoku can be found in surfing museums.

Surfers rode wooden boards before the advent of polyurethane foam blanks.

else to promote the sport to the mainland. Freeth also was among the generation of Hawaiians who stood up instead of riding on their bellies. Furthermore, he pioneered riding across the wave's **face** instead of going straight into the shore. Freeth eventually became a California lifeguard. He even gained Kahanamoku-like recognition for rescuing a fisherman in pulsating surf off Venice Beach near Los Angeles. But he never had the

FIVE IMPORTANT NAMES OF THE EARLY YEARS OF SURFING

Tom Blake, a 1920s and 1930s innovator in California, also was a stunt double for Clark Gable. Blake introduced a keel, or fin, that made turning boards easier.

George Downing was a post–World War II big-wave rider in Hawaii. Downing was the first to ride waves once considered too large to try.

Phil Edwards, a graceful California surfer of the 1940s and 1950s, helped create a fluid surfing style.

Greg Noll, known as "Da Bull," is a famous big-wave rider. He is credited with being among the first to tackle the big waves of **Waimea Bay**. He later started a successful surf-board shop in southern California.

Dale Velzy is known as an innovator in the surfboard designs of the 1950s and beyond and influenced many of the great surfers who shaped the sport's culture.

drawing power of Duke, a two-time Olympic champion at the 1912 and 1916 games and later a character actor in silent films.

Between Freeth and Kahanamoku, the sport caught on in California as much as in Hawaii. For the next thirty-five years, though, surfing remained an extremity of established sport with watermen/ waterwomen riding heavy redwood boards carved by hand and braving frigid water temperatures in the mainland without the benefit of wetsuits.

A NEW WAVE

When America seemed to change overnight after World War II ended, surfing was about to undergo a revolution too. California surfers became some of the sport's most creative innovators, introducing advances in surfboard manufacturing, gear, and fashion. Many of these innovators settled in southern California communities and Santa Cruz in central California, where today

those enclaves remain at the forefront of surfing originality.

A few personalities stand out; Bob Simmons, for example, who has been credited with introducing the mechanical design concepts used to build the modern-day **longboard**. Simmons, who suffered from cancer as a child and later was injured by a car while riding a bicycle, never was much of a surfer. But now the California Institute of Technology considers him to be one of its most decorated former students for his contributions to surfing. Simmons was at the forefront when plastics and polyure-thane materials were introduced to board building.

Lightweight polyurethane foam **blanks** were hand shaped, sanded, and coated in resin-hardened fiberglass to make smooth-gliding boards. Simmons worked with **shaper** Joe Quigg to create some of the first fiberglass boards, which were lighter than their redwood counterparts. That made them easier to transport and more attractive to more beachgoers, which, in turn, helped lead to a rise in popularity. The board manufacturing system they mastered lasted for a half century.

BECOMING MAINSTREAM

It wasn't until the late 1950s that surfing became a national craze. Board design was one reason, but advances in surfing photography also played an important role. Just as Jack London's words had done a half century earlier, vivid photos of surfers on large waves embodied a romantic pose that Americans embraced. Surfing seemed like an untamed frontier that fed the country's thirst for adventure. Some sources credit a 1953 Associated Press photo of surfers riding a big wave at Makaha, a famous locale on the island of Oahu, as piquing interest in Hawaiian surf. Thus began an exodus of mainlanders who challenged themselves on

Going right at the Hook in Santa Cruz, California

waves bigger and more powerful than those found along the California coastline.

Although these surfers have remarkable résumés for their contributions to the sport's growth, they might have flown under the radar if not for filmmaker Bud Browne. His surfing documentaries became legendary and played before rapturous, albeit local, audiences in high school gymnasiums near the beach. These garage films left an indelible imprint on the sport that led to interest from Hollywood.

Everything changed in 1959 with the Hollywood movie **Gidget**. Over the next five years, surfing enjoyed a prominent place in popular culture with its distinct music (Dick Dale), fashion (stripes), and film (*Beach Blanket Bingo*). The sport grew exponentially as once-empty beaches suddenly overflowed with surfers. It was another Brown, Bruce Brown, who brought an unvarnished version of the sport to the heartland. In 1966, he produced *The Endless Summer,* a tale of California surfers Robert August and Mike Hynson traveling the world looking for the perfect wave. With the vibrato sounds of surf music in the background and an artfully overlaid narration, the film depicted surfing as a capricious, youth-oriented activity. The country was enthralled.

SURFING GROWS UP

Benign times at the beach would fade quickly as the realities of the Vietnam War punctured holes in the innocence and confidence of the American psyche. The world changed in the late 1960s, and again surfing did too. The tumultuous period ushered in a revolution in board design. Whereas the 1950s and early 1960s celebrated the longboard era, this epoch introduced boards as

FIVE IMPORTANT NAMES OF THE 1960s

Hobie Alter, an Orange County surfboard shaper and entrepreneur, turned a garage industry into a thriving business.

Miki Dora, from **Malibu** and known as "Da Cat," was the ultimate outlaw surfer and helped create a mystique around the sport. When he died in 2002, he was considered influential for being a nonconformist.

Mike Doyle, a San Diego County surfer, was considered the best all-around waterman of the 1960s. He embraced all aspects of surfing, from paddle boarding to tandem surfing.

Mickey Muñoz of Orange County established surfing styles and surfboard design. He was among the first to ride the big waves of Oahu, and he was the stunt double for Sandra Dee in the movie *Gidget*.

Nat Young of Australia was the 1966 world champion. He helped usher in the **shortboard** era, as well as the competitive spirit of professionals from Down Under.

FIVE IMPORTANT NAMES OF THE 1970s

Eddie Aikau of Hawaii was one of the greatest watermen of all time. He was lost at sea in 1978 while paddling his surfboard to get help after a crew was stranded in an outrigger canoe.

Ian Cairns was one of the Bronzed Aussies who helped start a worldwide professional tour. Cairns understood the responsibility pro surfers had in creating a tour that considered their needs.

Corky Carroll, an Orange County champion, was known for bringing professionalism to the sport and as a recording artist and media star.

Margo Godfrey Oberg, Californian-turned-Hawaiian surfing champion, was one of the greatest women surfers of any era.

Shaun Tomson, a South African surfing champion, had style and grace and remained an influential figure past his prime.

much as three feet shorter, narrower, and lighter. The shorter boards allowed for more skateboard-like stunts on the wave's face, thus radicalizing the way people surfed. Surfing also lost its mainstream innocence with aficionados becoming as much a part of the counterculture as San Francisco hippies. The sport attracted sandal-wearing longhairs who munched granola and smoked pot, but it also saw the seeds of a structured sporting event begin to germinate.

Competitive-minded Australians provided a counterpoint to the hippie surfers of California and Hawaii. Promoters of popular surfing contests joined forces to form a world tour that today has stops in Australia, Brazil, California, France, Fuji, Hawaii, South Africa, and Tahiti. Media depicted these tournaments as exotic, borderline events practiced with acrobatic expertise. Mostly, though, television broadcasters liked the cringe factor they elicited by broadcasting fantastic **wipeouts** and an "agony of defeat" reaction from its audiences.

No wave produces a better viewer response than the Banzai **Pipeline** on the North Shore of Oahu. The wave breaks over a shallow coral reef, forming gigantic walls of water that cascade into cylinders big enough to drive a semitruck through. It became the star of surfing in the early 1970s. The ones who mastered this freight-train wave were idolized. None was better in the 1970s than Hawaiian Gerry Lopez, whose tube riding was legendary. He would disappear into the cresting pipelike wave before safely resurfacing into the sunlight as the nasty wave spit him out in a spray of mist. Lopez marketed his own Lightning Bolt line of boards and clothes. Even as he became a professional athlete, he never lost his laid-back Hawaiian roots, thus bridging the chasm between commercialism and the ancient Hawaiian rite of surfing.

FASHION STATEMENT

When surfing became more professional in the 1980s, commercialism gained a toehold. The sales of surf wear and gear allowed manufacturers to sponsor athletes who suddenly could make decent livings off their trade. A big part of it was surf fashion.

Surfing had introduced the casual look that influenced Californian and Hawaiian styles for decades. At first it was a matter of function: Jeans, t shirts, and tennis shoes fit the active lifestyle. The beach fashions eventually reached the heartland and Europe because they represented a dream of sunshine, cresting waves, and youthful, bronzed bodies. During this decade, quintessential surfers with their blond locks and trim physiques were plucked off the beach and splashed across spreads in high-fashion magazines.

Since the early 1980s, surfers-turned-fashion designers have continued to make a huge imprint on worldwide trends, with such brands as Quiksilver, Mossimo, Roxy, and Rusty finding their way to stylish boutiques. The multimillion-dollar enterprises owe a debt of gratitude to Walter and Phillip Hoffman, who were among the first to challenge the big **barrels** of the North Shore of Oahu. They also were part of the gang who helped create modern boards. Walter's stepdaughter, Joyce Hoffman, was a surfing star in the 1960s. The Hoffmans' work with fabrics has garnered them the most recognition. They took over their father's southern California textile business and eventually supplied most of the fabrics used by the surfwear industry. Surfing's worldwide image

FIVE IMPORTANT NAMES OF THE 1980s AND 1990s

Lisa Anderson, a Floridian, was considered the best female surfer in the 1990s but also was known for marshaling the women's surfing movement. She helped create stylish **board shorts** for women and surfed with more power than any woman previously.

Shane Dorian, from Hawaii's Big Island, never was the best contest surfer because he lacked a killer instinct. Still, fellow surfers consider him one of the greatest all-arounders of his generation. He was known for his **aerials** and tube rides.

Bob McKnight, chief operating officer of surf clothing manufacturer Quiksilver, based in Costa Mesa, California, is a trend-setting industry leader.

Mark Richards, from New South Wales, helped usher in the new generation of prolific surfers from Australia. Between 1979 and 1982 he won four consecutive world championships. He also popularized the **twin-fin** surfboard that showcased his dazzling skill.

Kelly Slater is perhaps the consummate pro surfer. He is a six-time world champion and continues competing successfully on the world tour. The Cocoa Beach, Florida, native is known for his ability to adapt to different wave conditions. He is one of the world's best-known surfers, even today.

Surf shops sell boards, gear, accessories, and clothing.

greatly increased through the branding of the clothes.

NEW FRONTIERS

As surfing rolled into the twenty-first century, surfers continued to seek new thrills. Some of the most intrepid individuals began challenging fifty-foot and higher waves. Not that long ago, these behemoth waves were considered too dangerous to ride, but surfers such as Hawaii's Laird Hamilton and Buzzy Kerbox perfected the art, borrowed from water skiing, of being towed into giant surf by personal watercraft, such as **Jet Skis**. Now known as **tow-in surfing**, this allowed them to get a head start on fast-moving waves and opened surfing to virtually every wave out there.

Beyond traditional surfing, the sport has spawned offshoots that wave riders also enjoy: Kite surfing combines surfing with windsurfing, and skateboarding and

FIVE IMPORTANT NAMES OF THE EARLY 2000s

Layne Beachley is a five-time world champion from Australia and is considered the best female big-wave surfer of all time.

Jeff Clark, who rode **Mavericks** in northern California alone for fifteen years, helped popularize big-wave surfing through his contest at the **epic** Half Moon Bay break. Clark is also a noted board shaper who owns the Mavericks Surf Shop not far from the break he put on the map.

Randy French is a Santa Cruz, California, surfer who has helped revolutionize surfboard production by introducing lightweight, mass-produced epoxy boards.

Andy Irons is a Kauai surfing champion with an explosive style in the water and on land, which has made him a media star. Irons's younger brother, Bruce, is also talented, and the sibling rivalry has been fodder for the surf press.

Stacy Peralta helped introduce the surf culture of the twenty-first century with the movies *Riding Giants* and *Dogtown.* He is a former professional skateboarder and surfer and was one of the "Z-Boys," the famous Santa Monica, California, skateboarders/hell-raisers.

Jeff Clark named his surf shop Mavericks, after the famous wave he helped discover.

snowboarding are natural extensions of surfing, practiced on asphalt and snow. Each variation enjoys its own following and organization.

DESIGN ADVANCES

One of the most important moments of the early twenty-first century involved the evolution of surfboard manufacturing. What had been an artisan profession since the days of Bob Simmons and Hobie Alter leaped into automation because of a strange event. On December 5, 2005, Gordon "Grubby" Clark closed his Clark Foam plant in Orange County without advance notice. The sudden demise of a surfing institution sent shock waves throughout the shaping industry because Clark provided 90 percent of the blanks used to make surfboards. After initial fears, insiders began viewing the mysterious dissolution of Clark Foam as advantageous for surfboard manufacturing. Clark, who had a monopoly, discouraged experimentation from competitors. He would punish anyone who tried to branch out by withholding blanks from them. His departure introduced new blank makers into the market and opened the industry to use more ecologically friendly materials.

CHAPTER 2

A surfer surveys the break above Steamer Lane in Santa Cruz, California.

Gear to Go

"He's in the barn," Cecelia Harrison said, pointing toward the back of the 200-year-old adobe in the remote hills of San Juan Capistrano, California, "waiting for you." I ambled past the rolling, sunbaked dirt until I found Lorrin "Whitey" Harrison fiddling with something inside the rickety barn. The space was stuffed with surfboards, outrigger canoes, and other accoutrements of surfing's rich past. (At Harrison's funeral service in 1993, *Surfer's Journal* publisher Steve Pezman described the disheveled contents of the barn as the "detritus of surfboard technology.") The barn symbolized the advancement of surfing, much like the Palo Alto garage of Bill Hewlett and Dave Packard had done for Silicon Valley. Some attribute the beginnings of polyurethane foam surfboards to Harrison, who in 1931 worked for a Los Angeles home builder that sold the first commercial surfboard.

The day I visited in the late 1970s, Harrison looked as weathered as an old stand of white ash. He wasn't wearing his signature palm-frond hat, instead letting a thatch of white curls swirl in the summer breeze. He recounted how he had learned to surf at his family's summer home in Laguna Beach in the early 1920s. He had met Duke Kahanamoku while surfing in Corona del Mar and was among the surfers who helped the famous Hawaiian to rescue drowning victims of the *Thelma* in 1925. Despite his surfing exploits, Harrison's reputation was cemented by his experimentation in the garage.

Harrison's innovative spirit is alive today where evolving technology has turned board building on its head. New composite materials and assembly-line production have led to lighter, easy-to-paddle boards. There has been no better time to learn to surf because of this refinement. The latest boards of nine feet and longer provide the buoyancy and stability needed to learn, but they're not as unwieldy as the 100-pound ancestor redwoods of Harrison's era.

THE SURFBOARD

Selecting a suitable board is one of the most basic decisions to be made when learning to surf. My first surfboard was a homemade seven-footer as red as cherry pie, with a turned-up, spiky **nose** and rock-hard side **rails**. It was, to put it politely, not the ideal beginner's board. Who knew? It's not easy to decide what to get with countless boards available and conflicting opinions on which ones work best. Local surf bodegas often are full of colorful characters with heaps of knowledge, but they aren't Saks Fifth Avenue. The sales help can be intimidating with its curious vernacular and too-cool aloofness. Buyers need to arm themselves with information before beginning their search.

In the most rudimentary sense, surfboards are of two types: shortboards and longboards. Each type has special features that make it distinct: one fin or tri-fins, soft rails or hard, pointy nose or round. All boards, however, are generally described by the proportions of their thickness, length, and width.

Here are some basic terms worth knowing:

Deck: The top of the board on which surfers stand or paddle. The surface is flat or slightly concave, and it's coated in wax for better grip.

Fin: The skeg, or keel-like hardened plastic attached to the rear bottom of the board; acts as a rudder. The length, thickness, and number of fins help determine how the board reacts when turning.

Foil: Measures the thickness of a board as it changes from nose to **tail**. The thickest part of the board usually is in the center. Foil is closely related to the board's **rocker**.

Handmade surfboards are built in "shaping rooms."

Nose: The front of the board. It's often a V-shaped point in shortboards and a blunt-shaped tip in longboards. Differences in nose design help determine the board's overall performance capability.

Rails: The sides of the board from tail to nose. Rails are crucial to the board's performance and are available in varying degrees of hardness. The harder the rail, the theory goes, the faster the surfboard will skim across a wave. The rails are thin at the nose and tail, and thicker in the center. Like other parts of the board, rails have a peculiar idiom, such as round rails, rolled rails, and **egg** rails.

Opposite: Surfboards come in a variety of sizes and shapes.

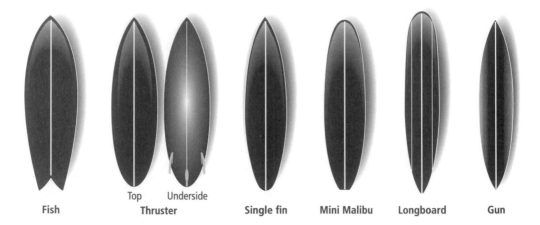

| Fish | Top   Underside | Single fin | Mini Malibu | Longboard | Gun |
| | Thruster | | | | |

Popular board designs. *Fish, Thruster, Single Fin, Mini Malibu, Longboard, Gun*

Rocker: The amount of rocker, or bend in the board from tail to nose, determines how loose and fast the board rides on the wave. A stiffer board can displace water better by creating less drag. A looser board turns more easily but doesn't plane efficiently. Most surfers try to find the perfect marriage of maneuverability and speed, which has led to continuous experimentation.

Stringer: Strips of wood built into the center of the foam blank of handmade boards to add rigidity from tail to nose. Stringers also give the shaper a landmark from which to make each side of the board the same. Many mass-produced boards don't have stringers, but they are more durable than handmade products.

Tail: The back tip of the board, which affects speed, drag, and turning ratio. Tails can be found in a variety of shapes. A few of the more popular shapes are roundtail, pintail, swallowtail, and wing.

HOW TO CHOOSE A BEGINNER'S BOARD

It's best to rent a beginner's board from a surf shop before buying one. By renting, you can experiment with different sizes, shapes, and materials and determine what feels right. The basic rule, though, is to get a longboard. A ten-foot-long board is a good length for someone weighing 180 pounds. According to Australian Ian Cairns, a 1970s champion who helped cultivate the professional surfing tour, the key is to get a bigger board than anyone recommends because balancing is really difficult: "The more buoyancy and support you have, the easier the chance to get a wave."

Another facet to consider is nose rocker. You don't need to get a radical design like I did many years ago, but you do need a board with extra rocker in the nose. This will help prevent **pearling**, in which the nose of the board dips under the water when you first

It's a good idea to wax your beginner's board before hitting the waves.

try but end up standing too far forward. There's not much else to worry about in the beginning. If you have a longboard with some nose rocker, you'll be in good shape.

SOFT FOAM VERSUS FIBERGLASS

You also must consider whether to start with a soft-foam board like the ones used in surf schools. These big boards are durable and have spongy decks that reduce the chance of injury. One of the most popular is the Surftech Softop, which has soft decks and rails but a fiberglass bottom that makes it more efficient. The best reason to start on a soft board is safety. (*Note:* Where there's hard fiberglass, there's greater risk of injury.) Because beginners don't have control, loose boards become a danger to everyone in their wake. Soft boards are perfect for the first few months, but eventually you will want to graduate to something that performs better.

THE NEXT STEP

Sometimes it seems board styles change as often as the clothes paraded down the famous runways in New York, Paris, and Milan. Before buying, it's best to know what you want from surfing. For some, easy paddling and cruising on a longboard will be enough. Others will want to advance to shortboards so they can perform tricks. Still others will want to challenge themselves in the biggest waves the ocean generates. Each circumstance requires a different type of board, as explained in the following sections.

LONGBOARDS

Longboards have the most basic shape, including a wide nose and tail. They are nine feet or longer and quite stable. Because of their size, they are made for skimming the wave without having to perform a lot of

Taking the longboard out to ride on a small day.

jerky, skateboard-type tricks. These boards, known as **logs**, are used for **nose riding**, where surfers work their way to the front tip and balance their toes over the front edge—hence, the terms **hanging ten** and **hanging five**.

When longboards were again in vogue in the 1990s, shapers got the idea to create them with more maneuverability by using the lightweight materials that had become available. That style of board is now known as the *mini-mal,* short for Malibu, the iconic L.A. beach. Mini-mals are more streamlined than classic longboards and often have multiple fins to provide better turning ratio while retaining their buoyancy for paddling. They also function as beginner boards, and they will be worth keeping once you progress. Many experts say mini-mals are a good buy for a first board.

SHORTBOARDS

Master surfers should be able to ride any style of board at most breaks, but they sometimes need a day to adjust to a new board's personality. Each board has a distinct feel because of the way it's curved and how it torques when meeting the moving wave. Because each break creates different kinds of waves, surf shops offer a variety of shortboards. Often these designs have subtle differences, which lead to raging debates about what works best. To help navigate through the minefield of design-speak, form a relationship with a local shaper where you expect to surf regularly. This shaper will have studied the nuances of the specific break and

Shortboards came into style in the late 1960s.

have figured out, basically, which designs work best there.

The evolution of shortboards is one of continual experimentation and refinement. Even though shortboards can be categorized into three styles—single fin, the Fish, and Thruster tri-fin—all have design variations within the genre. Once you reach an advanced level you will want to experiment to refine your style.

Shortboard Designs

Single-fin boards are basic solid designs that originated in the 1970s. They range from 6.25 to 7.5 feet in length. They come in varying shapes from nose to tail to rail but remain one of the most functional boards made because they work well in big and small surf.

The Fish has a potato-chip shape with a split-V tail. Which is also called a swallowtail. It's a twin-fin board with a round nose and a wide tail that's designed for smaller, slower surf. It was the forerunner of the twin-fin.

A **Thruster** is the original tri-fin developed in 1981 by Australian Simon Anderson. It remains popular today because it has the performance capabilities of the twin-fin but the stability of single-fin boards. Thrusters are sleek, thin, and paper light.

The Fish was an early twin-fin surfboard design.

A gun is on display at Mavericks Surf Shop, near one of California's biggest breaks.

GUNS

Guns haven't changed much in design over time because they're made to paddle into fast-charging giants and hold an edge during those thirty-foot **elevator drops**. Nothing fancy here—not when trying to survive. Guns are ten feet long, twenty inches wide, and thick with pointy noses and tails. They are called guns, or **rhino chasers**, in an obvious euphemism that draws a parallel to big-game hunters.

TOWBOARDS

Towboards are for waves so big you must be towed into them because paddling is ineffective; the motorized watercraft gives you a running start to catch a big wave. Since you aren't paddling, you don't require a gun's girth. Towboards are 3.5 feet shorter than guns, thus allowing surfers to carve turns instead of trying to outrun the big breakers. Like sailboards, towboards often have foot straps that aid in balance and maneuverability.

A NOTE ON FINS

Original wood boards didn't have fins until surf pioneer Tom Blake experimented with a metal boat keel on a paddleboard in 1935. Once the shortboard revolution hit, designers began experimenting with fins as much as other parts of the board. According to Matt Warshaw's *The Encyclopedia of Surfing,* a debate ensued in the late 1970s over the use of

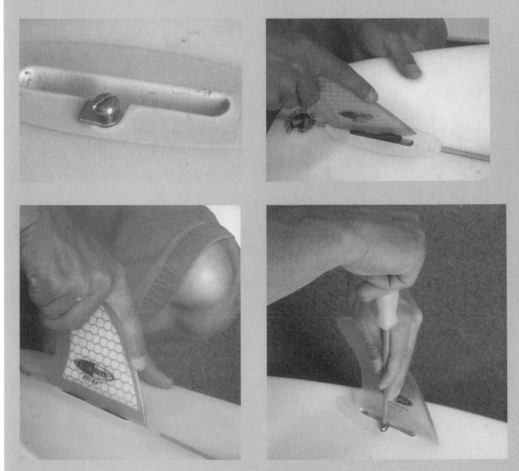

Fins can be inserted or removed with the help of a screwdriver.

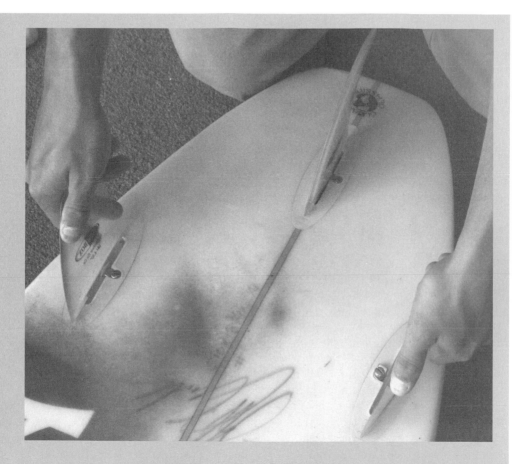

twin fins. Single fins provided more stability and, thus, control, especially when the waves reached six feet or higher. Some traditionalists dismissed twin fins, popularized by Aussie surfing star Mark Richards, as too unstable in big surf.

As surfboard manufacturing improved, surfers realized the importance fins play in control. Fins were originally permanently attached to the board with coats of fiberglass. By the late 1960s, however, they had started experimenting with removable fin systems. Now many shortboards come equipped with bolt-in fin systems, and boards can utilize as many as six fins.

MOLDED BOARDS

The one element of surfing that is constant is the continual change in equipment. The latest revolution in surfboard manufacturing involves mass production. The origins can be traced to Randy French, a Santa Cruz, California, shaper who has experimented with molded composites since the 1970s and formed Surftech. He borrowed the idea from sailboard technology, which has successfully used **molded boards** for years. French's company has pioneered the innovation of surfboard manufacturing in its Cobra plant in Thailand. Surftech boards are churned out assembly-line style. The company makes a board of **expanded polystyrene (EPS)**—the foam plastic used as protective packaging around boxed computers and other appliances—which is said to be stronger and lighter than traditional polyurethane foam blanks. EPS blanks are coated with epoxy instead of the layers of fiberglass found in handcrafted products. French, who started the company in 1989, purchased and uses the design **templates** of some of surfing's most venerable shapers, such as Dale Velzy, Reynolds Yater, and Mickey Muñoz, to mass-produce his boards.

Some say the molded boards are better built than the originals. But purists have rejected them, saying they are too light, ride too high on the wave, and have what is known as **chatter**, a description of how **bumpy** a board planes across a wave. If you've ever been in a speedboat on a windy day, you understand the concept.

The new system of production is ending an era of specialists who built boards by hand. "The surfboard as we knew it is dead, but there are niche brands that will survive off niche markets," said Dan Mann, director of research and design for Firewire Surfboards, a southern California company that builds composite boards.

CARING FOR YOUR BOARD

The odds of avoiding **dings**—surfers' jargon for nicks, cuts, cracks, breaks, tears, punctures, or dents in the surfboard's fiberglass coat (**glasscoat**)—are as slim as finding waves in your backyard swimming pool. Sometimes they happen nowhere near the water, when a board leaning against a wall crashes onto the floor or a surfer bumps it into a door. Mostly, though, dings occur when slamming into rock, coral reefs, jetties, piers, or another board.

Because some dings are the result of inattention, it's important to develop good habits when storing boards. For example, a cloth board bag is a good investment. Building and using storage racks in a garage can also extend a surfboard's life. Never leave a board lying around or in a space where something could fall on it, run over it, or otherwise damage it.

Most dings should be repaired before paddling out again. The fiberglass coat is meant to keep the board watertight; a hole allows absorption, which makes the board heavy and discolors it. Covering a minor tear with duct tape is acceptable in a pinch, but it's not a permanent fix.

Most popular breaks are home to surf

shops that handle ding repairs. The work is expensive and takes time because it's usually done by some guy out of his garage. That's reason enough to learn the basics of repair. Most surf shops and hardware stores sell basic repair kits.

The worst dings occur when the fiberglass membrane is penetrated and the foam core is gouged. It's worth considering professional repair in such cases unless you have experience and confidence in doing craftwork.

Repairing dings can be quite involved, depending on the type of board that is damaged. It's important to know what type of foam blank you have and to use the ingredients recommended in repair kits. A basic kit includes a fiberglass cloth, resin, sandpaper, a sanding block, and Q-Cell filler, a powdery thickening substance.

How to Fix a Ding

- Work in a shaded area. Ideally, use a padded, U-shaped shaping rack to attend to the ding. A table saw or some other stand that is padded and stable will suffice. Carefully lay the board on the stand.
- Cut away the cracked fiberglass skin with an X-Acto knife or razor blade. Allow the foam core to dry completely. Remove any damaged foam, and make sure the area around the ding is clean before proceeding.
- Cut a piece of fiberglass cloth roughly the size and shape of the area needing repair.
- Use the proper resin for the type of surf-

board being fixed. Polyester and epoxy resins are available. An easy way to determine which to use is to put a piece of foam in acetone; if it dissolves, use epoxy; if not, use a polyester resin.
- Create a border around the hole with masking tape. Then pour resin filler into the cavity until it reaches the level of the fiberglass membrane. Generally, you should make a medium-thickness Q-Cell filler (or similar resin filler) paste, but the consistency of the filler depends on the size of the ding.
- Place the precut fiberglass cloth over the hole, and let it dry as the resin hardens.
- Once the resin is dry, add a sanding coat of resin and trim away excess cloth.
- Allow the sanding coat to dry completely before sanding the surface to its original smoothness. Perfectionists often add a gloss coat and then buff it out with rubbing compound. Some also add pigments into the final coat to restore the board's original color.

THE ACCESSORIES

The image is intoxicating. A lean, bronzed surfer in floral-fabric board shorts or bikini stands at the edge of the shore, surfboard in tow. It creates the perception that, when stripped of its commercialism, surfing is free of adornment. "You don't really need a wetsuit or a surf leash or even trunks. All you really need is a surfboard and wax," pro surfer and author Sam George once told the *Los Angeles Times*.

THE SHAPER

John Mel is a throwback to surfing's nostalgic past. As a master surfboard builder, known around the beach as a shaper, his art is threatened by mass production and globalization. After four decades of handcrafting surfboards in a niche enterprise, Mel faces extinction as the industry undergoes considerable transformation. Until the late 1990s, Mel and his small cadre of craftspeople provided the majority of boards that were being used. An estimated 80 percent of boards sold in the United States were hand shaped through a labor-intensive method of refining a chunk of snow-white foam into sleek, fiberglass vessels. The drawn-out process involved glassing, sanding, **hot coating**, and cutting fin boxes. The materials and techniques of board building hadn't changed much since the 1950s. Within a decade, however, the number of handmade boards decreased to less than 20 percent as new companies found cheap labor on overseas assembly lines.

Board building has been an integral part of surfing's colorful culture. The garage shaper was a mixture of neighborhood bartender and family carpenter. When Mel, owner of Freeline Designs, crafted my first custom board in 1973, I sat in his shaping room among the cow pastures of 41st Avenue in Santa Cruz. With a blizzard of foam swirling in the air, we talked about the subtleties of my board, such as the rocker, the rails' thickness, and the swallowtails. We also talked about our lives. Mel knew my surfing ability and my goals, which helped him to design a board that provided the best possible experience.

While growing up in Hollywood Riviera, a stretch of coastal hills in suburban L.A., Mel started shaping out of his dad's garage. He eventually attended San Diego State and spent a summer apprenticing for pioneers Gordon & Smith Surfboards in San Diego. Mel took his craft to Santa Cruz in 1969 and established himself as one of the area's major shapers. His son, Peter, later became recognized as one of the world's great big-wave riders while surfing the famous Mavericks break 50 miles up the Pacific Coast.

Mel's hair has turned to the color of foam flecks. He still wears floral Hawaiian shirts, cargo pants, and sandals to work, and he loves making 250 to 300 boards a year.

Although Mel moves like an artist while sculpting the foam, he hasn't resisted technological advances. He uses computer-assisted designs for about half of his boards. The computer has eliminated the use of a Skil 100 door planer to trim the blocky foam blank. Now it's done with precision via a computer-generated cutter, and Mel uses his handy Skil 100 for detail work. The computer has upped production at least fivefold, Mel says.

With each custom board requiring ten to fifteen hours of labor, shapers don't make much money for the amount of time they put in. Anything to decrease the time is welcome, even by someone who is a tangible reminder of the roots of surfboard building.

John Mel, owner of Freeline Designs, shapes about 300 boards per year at his factory in Santa Cruz, California.

Surfing isn't as equipment oriented as cycling, skiing, and climbing. But like many recreational activities, innovative products have been created to enhance the experience. As the sport became more mainstream, safety features were introduced. And while the unspoiled portrait of the stripped-down surfer is alluring, some accessories have become as essential as the board itself.

WETSUITS

When dressing in a stretchy piece of fabric that protects the body from the water's chill, it's difficult to remember a time when surfers entered the ocean with little more than bathing suits. The wetsuit, which first was introduced to surfers in the 1950s, has opened the sport around the world. Although surfing is marketed to the mainstream as a summertime activity, the best waves are generated by big winter storms.

Wetsuits have allowed the intrepid to search out these waves even in such refrigerated lands as Alaska.

The early wetsuit was thick, bulky, and confining—difficult to put on and even harder to peel off when cold and wet. Advances in neoprene, however, have led to greater comfort and flexibility in the water. Today's suits are offered in a variety of sizes and thickness, from two to six millimeters. Companies such as Roxy make suits specially designed for women. Velcro has replaced zippers on some models, making them even easier to wear.

HOW TO BUY A WETSUIT

Many manufacturers make wetsuits. It's best to try on a variety of brands to get a sense of which cut feels best to you. From there, make sure you find one that fits correctly. Test the comfort by stretching your

New material makes it easier to put on and remove wetsuits.

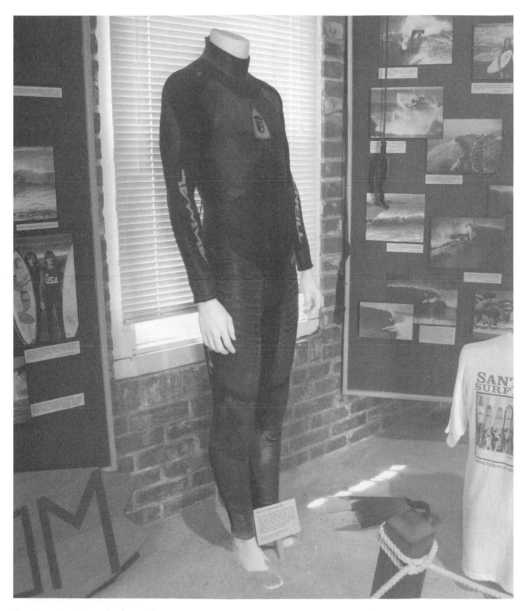

A prototype wetsuit, from the 1970s, is on display at the Santa Cruz Surfing Museum.

Booties and hoods provide extra protection from cold water.

arms overhead and bending over to touch your toes. Do some knee bends as well. The suit shouldn't feel too tight when doing these simple exercises.

Although wetsuits should be skintight to stop water from penetrating, you don't want yours to be so small that it constricts blood flow. No matter how well you care for it, neoprene eventually will stiffen. Most shops have size charts and salespeople to help guide you.

First-time buyers should find a durable suit that has the right thickness (protection against the cold) for the spot where you regularly surf. If you're surfing in only warm climates, a vest and spring suit might suffice. If you surf in colder climes, you should get something thick enough to make your stay in the ocean enjoyable. Most surfers will gladly offer advice on matters of thickness and wetsuit style, so it's useful to ask around at your local break.

Some additional wetsuit accessories are invaluable. Booties, for example, not only keep the feet warm and dry, but they also protect surfers from the sharp edges of rocks and coral reefs. **Hoods** and gloves are also sold for extreme cold-water surfing.

Basic Rules for Wetsuit Maintenance

Wetsuits should be cleaned in freshwater after each use because salty water causes deterioration. Also, leaving a smelly wetsuit around the house will not endear you to friends and loved ones. Here are a few tips for wetsuit care:

■ Turn the suit inside out and rinse in freshwater after each use. Also, soak the suit in warm, but not hot, water for about fifteen minutes after each use. (Hot water can contribute to the deterioration of the fabric.)

■ Many experienced surfers keep plastic tubs in their vehicles in order to store dripping wetsuits after surfing. It's easier to wash a suit in a tub.

■ Keep your suit out of direct sunlight. Hang dry suits in shady places on wide wooden or plastic hangers, or fold and lay them flat in a safe place. Don't leave a suit crumpled up because that could weaken the material. And don't use a dryer or put a suit too close to a fire or heater.

■ Cleaning the suit regularly with baby shampoo or a special wetsuit shampoo will help reduce pungent odors. Some manufacturers warn against using anything other than these shampoos.

■ Fix small tears immediately with neoprene glue or other adhesives made for wetsuit repairs.

■ Apply a lubricant to the zippers occasionally so they don't rust.

■ Many advise against urinating in the suit. Not only does urine harm the fabric—its, uh, "distinct" odor is difficult to remove.

Manufacturers advise against urinating in wetsuits.

THE WETSUIT PIONEER

Jack O'Neill is not the agile surfer/sailor of yesteryear. He needs a hearing aid to catch conversations. He wears a black patch (to block out light) over his left eye, which was damaged in a surfing accident in 1971. But open the sliding glass door to his cliff-hugging home overlooking one of Santa Cruz's famous surfing locales, and O'Neill, well into his eighties, seems rejuvenated. He takes a big drag from the salty, fresh air and sighs. It takes him back a half century, to the frigid, dank beaches of San Francisco where he began his quest to design a wetsuit—a piece of gear as important to surfers as their boards. "When I started, surf was a dirty word," he said one autumn day while **clean** westerly **swells** crashed below his house. "The city thought those guys out there were a bunch of bums. They threatened to arrest them."

That was the late 1940s. At the time, O'Neill worked as a windows and skylight sales rep in San Francisco, but spent his lunch hour bodysurfing at the beach. He and a handful of hardy San Franciscans would congregate at Ocean Beach, where powerful currents, unruly swells, and freezing water make swimming hazardous. They ignored the signs warning people to stay out of the water. Unlike their counterparts in Hawaii and southern California, their biggest obstacle was braving the numbing cold. They bought wool sweaters and shirts at a Goodwill store. Some soaked sweaters in oil to repel water. They wore bun-hugger swimsuits they rented for twenty-five cents. To warm up on the beach, they made bonfires with driftwood and tires.

But these gutsy individuals could do little to avoid turning a freakish purple after just a half hour in the ocean. One surfer tried wearing a navy-issue sweater sprayed with waterproofing sealant. It didn't work, but the concept led O'Neill to his lifelong pursuit. He began looking in navy surplus stores for skin-diver equipment used in World War II. The cold-water surfers started wearing long underwear and a layer of rubber rolled over it. But the surf would pull it apart, or the two pieces of rubber wouldn't fit properly and would fill with water. One day, O'Neill found a piece of unicellular foam and made a diaper out of it. He found the material helped keep part of him warm. Next, he experimented with polyvinylchloride (PVC) foam, which pulled apart too easily, so he glued a thin sheet of plastic over it and made one of the first vests. Those early prototypes, though, absorbed too much water.

The breakthrough came in 1951 when University of California, Berkeley physicist Hugh Bradner used neoprene to invent the modern-day wetsuit. The synthetic rubberized material is flexible, lightweight, and doesn't tear in the surf. It also insulates the surfer by trapping body heat. O'Neill said he learned about neoprene from a friend. He began experimenting with the material, which would eventually revolutionize surfing. By 1952, O'Neill had made

Wetsuit pioneer Jack O'Neill on the deck of his home in Santa Cruz, California

some suits for his buddies. One told him, "You're going to sell to five guys on the beach, and then you're going to be out of business." Undaunted, he opened a store across from his Ocean Beach surfing haunt. The shop supplied surfers with wax, wetsuit vests, and **balsa** boards. O'Neill called his store Surf Shop because he offered more than boards.

The San Francisco surfers eventually started spending weekends seventy miles south of the city in Santa Cruz, where the surf was good. O'Neill relocated there in 1959 and used his business acumen to create an aura of mystique around his product by coining the slogan "It's always summer inside."

LEASHES

Pat O'Neill, son of Jack O'Neill, invented the leash or **cord** in 1970 out of necessity. He surfed at the inviting breaks below his father's cliff house in Santa Cruz, California. When surfers fell there, the boards rode the waves into the jagged cliffs, often tearing the boards' hulls or breaking them in two. Those surfers lucky enough to escape board damage still had a long swim to retrieve their **sticks**.

Pat O'Neill's original experiment involved nylon ropes, surgical tubing, and a suction cup. People thought it was a remote control, O'Neill once told a reporter. It didn't take long for O'Neill and others to develop more practical leg ropes that fastened to the ankle. However, not everyone endorsed them. Purists called leashes "kook cords," or worse. They said leashes allowed inexperienced surfers to attempt to surf breaks beyond their skills, adding to the

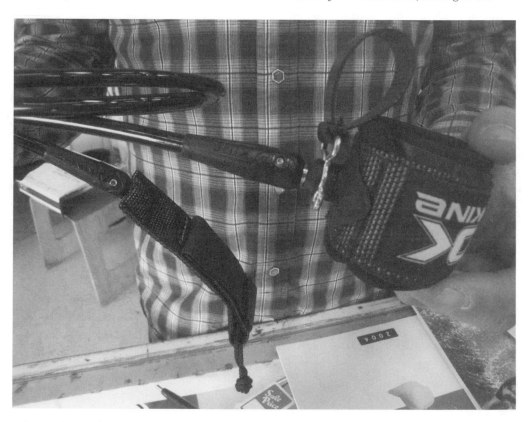

A leash with a safety release pin

danger of the sport. But within a decade, almost all surfers used them.

Leashes are sold in numerous sizes. Many come with little pockets that can hold car keys on the ankle strap. Most surfers prefer lightweight cords that are the length of their boards. Longboarders, however, generally use longer leashes. And those who ride the monster surf use longer, thicker cords to withstand the punishment. Leashes made for gigantic waves often come with a safety pin, which allows for quick releases when the leash gets wrapped around rocks and the surfer is being taken down by the wave.

Note: Leashes are not a substitute for being a weak swimmer. Never paddle into a situation that is beyond your ability. Leashes often break, and you must be able to swim in without relying on your board as a flotation device.

Modern leashes are pliable urethane **cords**

A slipped overhand knot is the proper knot for the leash string.

connected to a piece of nylon that helps protect the board's rails from the cord rubbing into them. A leash is attached at one end to the back ankle with a Velcro strap. A **leash plug** is drilled into the board's deck near the tail, where a leash is attached by nylon rope.

It's important to attach the leash correctly because you don't want to get tangled by it as you walk, paddle, or stand up. Attach the cord carefully, with it extending back from your ankle toward the tail, before heading into the water.

Surfboard leashes are usually sold with a piece of nylon string already tied into a knot. If not, make an overhand slip knot into a simple loop.

How to Attach the Leash to the Board

- Thread the loop end through the leash plug's metal bar. If that proves too difficult to accomplish, use fishing line or a screwdriver to push it through. If using a metal tool, be careful not to break the plug or gash the board. Also, make sure the knot is big enough so it won't slip through the plug when stretched.
- Once the string is through the bar, thread the other end through the loop to form a slip knot around the bar.
- Attach the rectangular rail saver by guiding it through the loop and fastening the strap. Make sure the string's knot is tucked inside the rail saver.
- When finished, hold down the tail of the board and give the leash a good tug to ensure it's fastened snuggly. If not, it could rip away from the board after a hard fall.

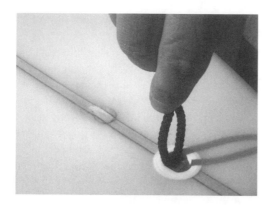

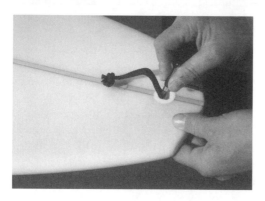

Thread the loop end through the leash plug's metal bar.

The Velcro strap connects to the board through the loop sticking out of the leash plug.

SURF WAX

The deck of a new surfboard is shiny, slick fiberglass. So they don't slip off easily, surfers need something to give them traction and repel water. What they discovered in the 1930s was paraffin wax. According to a letter he wrote to *Longboard* magazine, Alfred Gallant Jr. claimed credit for introducing paraffin wax to surfers. In 1935, Gallant, then a teenager living in Palos Verdes, California, borrowed his mom's liquid floor wax to coat his board after feeling his feet stick to the wooden floors. His mother chastised him for using her expensive cleaning product but also suggested he try paraffin wax, which she used to can fruits and jellies. The idea caught on, and surfers used paraffin wax for the next quarter century.

By the mid-1960s, some individuals had begun creating their own versions of surf wax by experimenting with oils mixed into the paraffin wax. This led to a softer, more

Many varieties of surf wax can be found.

Use a plastic wax comb to remove wax or rough up newly applied wax.

colorful, and easier-to-apply product than block-hard paraffin. As with other stories of industriousness in surfing, a few wax makers made it big over the next decade. One of the most popular products had the risqué name "Sex Wax." It was the brainchild of Rick Herzog of Goleta, California. Herzog, a onetime dishwasher, Disneyland ride operator, and groceries stocker, shaped surfboards in the late 1960s while earning an economics degree at UC Santa Barbara. A chemist worked in a building next to Herzog (who is now in his sixties). The two got to talking about the difficulties of using paraffin and came up with a formula for surfboard wax. The first batches seemed to work better than paraffin, but Herzog set aside his invention initially. In the early 1970s, Wax Research in southern California

launched a surf wax business that seemed to take off, so Herzog revisited his creation. A friend came up with the provocative name and entertaining logo. Herzog used tuna cans as molds, loaded cases of scented wax into his van, and solicited surf shops from Santa Cruz to San Diego. By the early 1980s, Sex Wax and Wax Research were each selling one million bars annually.

By the 1990s, wax makers had introduced new formulas considered superior to the original design in that they offered surfers better grip. Generally, surfboard wax includes petrochemicals such as petroleum jelly, paraffin wax, adhesives, polymers such as plastics, dyes for coloring, and perfume. Four basic types of wax are manufactured: *cold, cool, warm,* and *tropical.* The hardness of the wax depends on the ingredients. Hard wax is more adhesive and is used in warm-water conditions or as a primary coat. Softer waxes are used in colder water temperatures and as top coats.

Each surfer has his or her own system for applying wax. For example, Todd Johnson, a pro for the Mavericks Surf Shop in Princeton-by-the-Sea, California, likes to hold the bar loose in his hand and use only an edge, beginning with thin half circles across the deck. Others like rubbing the bar with a flat hand in a back-and-forth motion to create a thin, even layer. As long as the end result is a nicely waxed board, the exact method doesn't matter.

How to Wax Your Board

■ Find a cool or shady place to work.
■ Apply a layer of hard wax for the first

coat. Start at the tail and work your way toward the tip, which doesn't need to be waxed.

- Make sure that enough wax is applied to the areas where you normally place your feet. Also rub wax onto the top of the rails, especially where you normally push up when standing. Insufficient wax on the rails could lead to a bad wipeout on **takeoff**.
- Next, use a softer wax for the top coat. When rubbing in the top coat correctly, you will hear a buzzing sound over the deck.
- Apply a thick coat to start, especially if you are a beginner.
- Always add a fresh coat before surfing, but don't let old wax build up too much.
- Use a plastic comb, or wax remover device, to rough up the newly applied wax.
- In hot climates, wet the surface of the board before putting on the fresh top coat so it will stick better.
- Carry a chunk of wax in your board shorts or wetsuit in case you need to touch up your board while you're in the water.
- If you surf daily, remove old wax buildup a couple of times each month. If you live in warm climates, you can accomplish this easily by leaving your board on the beach on a hot day for ten minutes. When the wax becomes gooey, rub sand over it and wipe it off. Old wax also can be stripped with a plastic device with teeth or a wax remover. If you live in a colder climate you must use a solvent, such as Pickle Wax Remover, to maintain your board.

THE EXTRAS

It's possible to accessorize like a fashionista. How much to buy depends on how much and where you surf. The following are some products worth considering after the initial learning stages:

Deck grips attach to the deck of the board and offer traction, but they can cause discomfort while paddling. Some suggest beginners use only tail patches, which helps you place your feet to turn the board better. In a way, the tail patch serves as a compass by guiding you where to plant your feet when turning.

Rash guards are tight-fitting Lycra shirts that serve multiple purposes. They provide a comfortable layer under a wetsuit, and they also help warm-water surfers protect their skin from rubbing against the waxed board. In addition, rash guards protect skin against ultraviolet rays that are strong in summer or tropical surf spots.

Noseguards are soft, rubber devices for surfboards with pointed noses. They decrease the chance of injury in a collision and protect the board's tip, which is prone to chipping when transported or when hitting rock jetties or another board.

Racks are used by kayakers, skiers, and cyclists who need to transport their expensive toys safely. Racks have become big business, and surfers have benefited from this demand as major roof rack manufacturers Yakima and Thule now offer models for surfboards. Some manufacturers also sell straps to tie boards atop a vehicle. With so many styles now offered, it's best to

It is important to learn how to properly wax a surfboard.

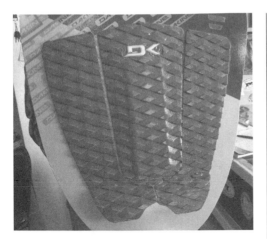

Deck patches are sometimes used instead of wax.

research what works for your vehicle. Each set of racks will come with instructions. It's better to follow those guidelines than to rely on something more general. Racks usually are fairly easy to install.

Wear a Lycra rash guard underneath a wetsuit.

TIPS FOR CAR TRAVEL

Containers: Use plastic containers to organize gear. One container is for the wet stuff, such as wetsuits and trunks or bikinis. Another is for fresh towels, and yet another is for extra leashes, wax, sunscreen, and the like.

Plastic jug of fresh water: Many remote locales don't have washroom facilities. Carry enough water to clean sand off your body, wetsuit, and board.

Plastic mat: Carry a mat to stand on while changing into and out of your wetsuit on asphalt.

Hair products: Some surfers I know carry a little container filled with conditioners and emollients to protect their sun-streaked hair after a session in salty water.

CHAPTER 3

The surfer is working the wave off the point at Steamer Lane.

The Ocean

The sea has captivated humans from time immemorial. Something about its vastness, its fluctuations, and its waves has inspired authors and poets dating back to Aeschylus's *Prometheus Bound,* but for diehard surfers the fascination with the sea often goes beyond the ethereal to the tactile. Not every surfer studies oceanography or marine biology, but many become amateur experts in the science of waves, and most have a healthy respect for sea life and marine flora and fauna. Much of their information is gathered anecdotally but with astute observation gleaned from years of on-the-ground experience. Nothing is more important to surfers than understanding waves.

"It's the whole ball of wax," says Ricky Griggs, famous pioneer surfer and professor emeritus of oceanography at the University of Hawaii. "You have to know about the ocean . . . not in a technical way, but you have to know it intuitively." He said many fellow surfers he has met "are magical oceanographers." Expert surfers know what the currents are going to do and at what tide. They know how **steep** it's going to be at a certain takeoff point, how the wind will affect the wave from every angle. They know what the direction of the **swell** will do to the waves at every break they frequent. They have to—or they'll miss out on some good action.

Before the introduction of online forecasting services such as Surfline.com, surfers developed their own methods to predict incoming swells. By monitoring subtle changes in ocean currents, weather patterns, and the like, they got to know their regular spots well enough to make reasonable guesses about the best months and seasons for surfing. Many of us believed that mid-October brought excellent fall surf to west-facing beaches along the southern

California coastline, but we never knew for sure—and that imbued the sport in a spirit of spontaneity.

Clearly, one cannot count on instinct or old wives' tales alone. The more wave knowledge you accumulate, the better you can accurately gauge when the good swells will come. No one knows this better than Sean Collins, a community college dropout who has become the world's best-known wave forecaster. Collins, who has surfed for almost five decades, studied marine charts while sailing with his father. He built his own database, and in 1984 he introduced the call-in line 976-SURF. He moved the service to the internet in the 1990s, and it has radically changed the way surfers check for waves. At Surfline.com you can click on any spot on the map of the oceans and discover when a swell will hit. The Friday I visited Collins, he showed me and my companions how a big swell would reach Indonesia by the following Wednesday, giving us plenty of time to catch those waves had we the money and inclination to do it.

Forecasters use up-to-the-minute data procured from weather satellites to follow storms thousands of miles from shore. They have scanned sources such as the Jet Propulsion Laboratory's (JPL's) SeaWinds Scatterometer and the National Aeronautic and Space Administration's (NASA's) QuikScat satellite, which can be found at the website of the JPL at the California Institute of Technology (www.jpl.nasa.gov). These sources provide detailed weather forecasts that can help you understand how climate is affecting the ocean in real time. While accurate information about weather is a mouse click away, serious surfers still must learn the basic principles of waves to get the most out of the information available on the web.

Riding back-side at Steamer Lane in Santa Cruz, California

WAVES

Many types of waves exist in the physical world, including sound waves, microwaves, and ocean waves. The **shape** of ocean waves is variable, depending on the wind, swell, tide, ocean floor, and coastline where the waves arrive. The best surfing waves rear up upon entering a surf zone, with the front forming a **curl** that cascades to the bottom, or **trough**, with a noise similar to the banging of cymbals. Just as often,

though, swirling winds flatten the waves before they reach the surf zone, resulting in **whitecaps** at sea—picturesque, perhaps, for impressionist painters but of little use to surfers as the wave spills over into a foamy white dome that can't be ridden.

When watching a big swell hit the shore in a last gasp of energy, it's difficult to imagine it accumulated across the ocean's expanse. One of the best descriptions of waves' origins comes from Steven Kotler's memoir, *West of Jesus:*

It started out in some other part of the world, forming when a change in temperature produced a change in pressure. Air's natural tendency is to move from an area of high pressure to an area of low pressure. We call this movement wind. When wind flickers across the ocean's surface, it produces small ripples which provide a greater surface area that can then catch more of that blowing wind. Eventually these ripples become larger and larger until they cohere into wavelets and eventually waves, attaining their greatest size when they come closest to matching the wind's speed. What makes this whole chain of events slightly stranger is that it is not the water itself traveling across the ocean as a wave, but merely the memory of the original wind's energy being constantly transferred as vibration from one neighboring water molecule to the next. When I heard the roar of that wave behind me at Nusa Dua, what I was actually hearing was the sound of the past arriving in the present with me directly in its path.

Wind is the primary factor in generating waves. Ocean storms create winds that in turn make ripples, or capillary waves, on the sea. The stronger the wind blows,

Dropping in late can be like riding a waterfall.

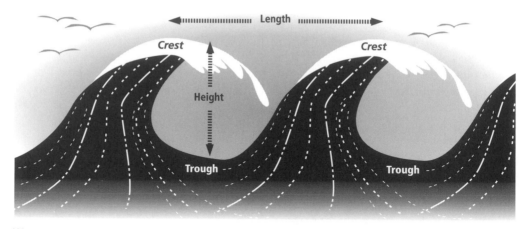

Wave measurements. *Wave height is the distance between the trough and the crest; the wave-length is the time it takes for a succession of waves to pass a point.*

the larger the capillary waves grow. These random waves eventually join other capillary conditions to create even larger waves. Farther away from the wind source, these waves develop into unbroken lines known as *wave trains* that can travel thousands of miles on their own. The fastest-moving waves lead the charge toward the coastline with the followers riding off their backs. As a result, they hit the surf breaks in **sets**.

The best kind of swell for surfing is a **groundswell**. (The other kind of swell is a **wind swell**; surfers call these *wind waves*. Wind waves often are **choppy** and unorganized and don't necessarily break over shallow bottoms conducive to perfectly shaped combers worth riding.) Groundswells usually have crossed the span of an ocean. The idea is that the longer the wavelength, the faster the waves will be moving. According to ocean-

ographers, the three factors that most affect wave size are wind speed, wind duration, and something known as **fetch**—the one-way distance over open water that wind travels to create waves. A simple equation is used to determine fetch: The hardest wind blowing over the longest time over the greatest distance (the fetch) brings the biggest waves.

Forecasters tracking major storms—say, from the Gulf of Alaska or Sea of Japan—also must know the physical traits of each break along the coastline to predict where the best surf will hit after calculating the wind's speed, duration, and fetch. They analyze tides and the topography of the ocean bottom, technically known as the underwater *bathymetry*. These elements are important because they greatly affect surfing conditions at each spot once the swell arrives.

TIDES

The gravitational pull of the moon and sun dictate the regular ebb and flow of the ocean's water level, usually in 12.5-hour cycles. Most breaks have two cycles per day, so it's important to monitor the peak high and low tides and know how the break reacts to each tidal change. Most surf shops carry small tide charts for their local breaks that measure these changes with pinpoint accuracy. Tides can be calculated years in advance, and the tables are infinitely useful. For example, some breaks only materialize at certain tides, meaning the window of opportunity each day is short. You must know the time of day when the tide will be high enough, or low enough, for the waves to break.

Anyone who has studied geography knows tides aren't the same at every beach. The Bay of Fundy in eastern Canada has the world's largest tide variations, with the level changing as much as fifty feet. The California coast varies by perhaps five feet. Tidal differences can greatly enhance or reduce the availability of good surf. Extreme tides occur when the moon and

Surfing is like a dance across the wave.

sun are aligned on the same side of Earth or on opposite sides. You must know how your break handles such situations because surfing everywhere changes drastically during extreme tides.

In general, low tides cause waves to **suck out**, or **peel**, quickly. This could provide optimal surfing conditions at a shallow reef break, or it could make the waves break too strongly at beach breaks. High tides cause waves to roll with a crumbling effect, which often is good for beginners. But the formula is not that simple. Tides are just one factor in the overall calculation of how waves break. In addition to the tide, you must consider the swell size, strength, and direction. And this formula works out dif-

ferently for almost every break. A high tide tends to handle a fast-moving groundswell better because it doesn't slow down the swell as much, but such tides also can flatten out smaller waves. A good rule to remember is that smaller breaks—the ones you'll probably use most for your first few years of surfing— improve on an outgoing tide because the lowering water level exposes the **sandbar**, reef, or point, that shapes the wave.

OCEAN FLOOR

Like the tides, the ocean floor greatly influences the wave as it spills over. Familiarize yourself with the undersea characteristics

A small, tubular wave breaks at low tide at a beach break.

Crumbling waves are good to ride when learning to surf.

of your regular break, such as sandy bottoms, reefs, and trenches. This not only will help you ride the best swells, but the knowledge will augment your ability to surf there safely.

To better understand the influences of the topography you must first learn about **shoaling**. When a swell hits shallower water near the coastline, the bottom of the wave drags along the ocean floor. It's as if the wave skids to a halt from the weight of an anchor. When this occurs, the wave's energy is pushed up, giving it more height. The steeper the slope of the bottom, the higher the wave reaches. But monster surf derives out of **deepwater breaks**. Because the islands of Polynesia are beyond the continental shelf, they absorb swells that

The construction of a small boat harbor in Newport Beach, California, wiped out a big break that once rolled into Corona del Mar.

have been unobstructed by land masses. When a wave coming out of deep water hits the bottom, it **jacks up** to tremendous heights. This phenomenon explains why Mavericks, the famous northern California big-wave surfing spot, can handle huge surf. The waves flow over deep water, then hit a rocky, jagged canyon that allows them to hold up even as they reach heights up to fifty feet.

The tides and ocean floor combine to form many types of waves. Some are preferred by expert surfers, whereas others are more conducive to beginners. The following are some basic wave formations:

Peeling waves often are described as

perfect to ride because they carry power as they peel along the reef, sandbar, or point, forming nicely shaped **shoulders** to maneuver.

Tubes are hard-breaking, top-to-bottom cylinders of water that are the ultimate experience for shortboarding as long as they hold up with a shoulder. If the tube is big enough, you can disappear completely behind the crashing curtain of water and then reappear as the force pushes you onto the shoulder.

Crumbling waves are slower moving, with the **crest** not quite forceful enough to peel over. The crest sort of peters out, or crumbles, into white foam. Beginners should try to find crumbling waves to get used to the motion of standing on a board.

Closeouts occur when the waves curl over simultaneously from crest to trough across the break. The wave doesn't have a gently sloping shoulder for riding beyond the crest. Closeout sets in large surf can be dangerous because you have nowhere to go but down when wiping out.

A closeout forces the surfer to straighten out instead of riding across the face.

TYPES OF BREAKS

Another major element that plays into what kind of wave you will encounter is the break. Surfers generally list six physical characteristics that make a break distinct: beach breaks, jetties, piers, points or headlands, reefs, and river mouths. Reefs and points generally provide fewer variables in wave shape and size. If the swell is coming from the northwest on a low tide, the wave probably will react in a specific way each time. Beach breaks, jetties, piers, and river mouths are less predictable because of changes in the ocean floor.

Beach breaks may offer plenty of room for beginners to practice.

Rock or concrete jetties, constructed to build small boat harbors or prevent beach erosion, often form good surfing waves.

BEACH BREAK

Beach breaks are among the safest spots to learn to surf because the waves break over sandy bottoms. Waves here are shaped by sandbars and channels carved by rip currents making their way back to sea. Many times you will find wide expanses of beach where the waves roll in, allowing plenty of room to practice, but beach breaks must be studied closely because oftentimes the bottoms aren't conducive to forming good waves. You often encounter closeouts, particularly at lower tides. Beach breaks also sometimes are more random than reefs and points because of shifting sandbars. That means they are more difficult to analyze until you arrive at the beach.

JETTIES

Beach breaks also are affected by rock pilings, which are erected at harbor mouths or, in the case of the Balboa Peninsula in Newport Beach, California, to fight beach erosion. **Jetties** are those loose boulders or concrete slabs that are built perpendicular to the shoreline. An unintended benefit of such **breakwaters** is that they create sandbars near their tips that can improve wave

The Wedge in Newport Beach, California, has one of the world's most famous bodysurfing waves.

quality. The sandbars form just to the right or left of where the **jetty** ends, and on a good swell at the right tide the waves break perfectly over the elevated ocean bottom.

The jetty also sometimes forms what is known as **reflected waves**. This happens when the wave bounces off the jetty and forms a wedge shape that is larger than the original wave. One of the world's most famous bodysurfing waves that exemplify this phenomenon is called **The Wedge**. This wave is formed when big south swells hit the jetty at the Newport Harbor mouth. Because the beach at the end of the jetty faces south, it absorbs direct hits from the strong, hurricane-generated swells. And after the swells slam into the jetty, the waves sometimes triple their height before crashing over a shallow sandy bottom. When The Wedge goes off, thousands cram the peninsula to watch bodysurfers and bodyboarders perform high-wire circus acts. More than a few daredevils have been carted away with broken necks.

PIERS

Piers often produce good waves on either side because sandbars have been created in response to deep channels underneath the pier. You must watch for some time to determine where the best sandbars are located. Unlike jetties, they are not necessarily only at the tip of the pier. A big pier can create multiple sandbars, giving surfers many choices of fine **peaks**.

POINTS OR HEADLANDS

A combination of a protruding landmass, a river mouth, and a rocky bottom can result in a classic **pointbreak**. When the waves hit the coastline at a point, they bend with the contour of the land to wrap around the point. On the right swell direction, the waves peel around the bend for long, sloping rides. Pointbreak waves usually are predictable and playful in small to medium surf.

Piers can create nicely shaped waves for surfing.

REEFS

Reef breaks provide some of the best surfing because elevated rocky reefs generally are more permanent than sandbars, which can disappear after a big storm. Rock or coral reefs form waves when waves travel from deep water to shallow water. When they shoal over a shallow reef, they often rise up, **pitching** out to form tubular waves, but not all reefs act this way. Whereas some create the world's fiercest waves, other reef breaks are gentle and great places for beginners. If you are not sure if a break is right for beginners, check with the local surf shop or lifeguard to find out where to go.

RIVER MOUTHS

River mouths deposit sand accumulations that help form the waves at beach breaks or point breaks. The river brings sand and dirt while emptying into the sea. These deposits build up to the left or right of the river mouth, and incoming waves break over them. Currents around river mouths are strong and unpredictable.

WIND DIRECTION

Wind direction is yet another part of the equation for finding good surf. The general rule is that windless conditions are ideal for preserving the wave's shape. Dawn and dusk are the best times to surf—depending on tides—because the winds tend to be calmer at those times of day. But some

Opposite: A rocky reef at Pacifica, California

breaks are protected by cliffs on both sides, which also helps to decrease windy conditions. You have a better chance of finding waves unaffected by wind at such spots. Most often, two types of wind are discussed: **onshore winds** and **offshore winds**.

ONSHORE WINDS

Winds blowing in from the ocean, known as onshore winds, ruin surfing conditions within minutes. The winds hit the top of waves and force them down, often before they have a chance to hit the underwater

Onshore winds wreak havoc on waves when it comes to surfing.

barrier that helps them break cleanly. The onshore winds also push the waves around unprotected breaks, making their arrival in the surf zone more sporadic and less organized. Gale-force onshore winds will form whitecaps, or boiling over, in the ocean before the waves ever reach the break.

OFFSHORE WINDS

A wind blowing from land toward the ocean, an offshore wind, can cause a **feathering** effect with a beautiful cloud of spray trailing off the wave's top. This improves the wave's shape for surfing because the curl doesn't immediately tumble to the trough. Instead, it forms a **pocket** that holds its form. Surfers usually prefer slight offshore wind conditions because when the wind blows too strong, it can be difficult to paddle down a wave's face.

THE LIVING SEA

The ocean is a wilderness. When entering it, you must treat it and its inhabitants with respect, especially when dealing with sharks, just as you would an Alaska wilderness populated by grizzly bear and wolves. Because of mass media preoccupation, the stealthy creatures that live just beneath the surface of the ocean personify the evil that lurks there.

Although shark attacks are rare, they receive great attention when they occur. Depending on where you live, you're probably going to encounter the mild sting of a jellyfish before ever seeing the fearsome

dorsal fin of a shark cruising in your direction. Fortunately, beginners don't have too many dangerous encounters other than with their own boards.

It seems the risk of getting bit, stung, or zapped increases exponentially the better you get, especially if you travel to exotic locales in search of surf. The box jellyfish and blue-ringed octopus in Australia, for example, can be fatal (even some of the seashells in Australia house deadly creatures). Sea snakes in Indonesia and Central America can result in rare bites. Then there are stingrays, stonefish, moray eels, sea urchins, and, yes, stinging seaweed. Familiarize yourself with all of these beings before jumping into their habitat.

SHARKS

Experts say four kinds of sharks attack humans on a statistically consistent basis: the white, tiger, bull, and oceanic white tip. Other dangerous breeds are makos, hammerheads, and blue-nosed sharks.

Tiger sharks present a danger in Hawaii's warm waters. They are famous for indiscriminately eating car license plates and whatever else they can find to munch. Bull sharks also are warm-water fish, patrolling the Gulf of Mexico and the Florida coastline. Yet nothing in the water presents a more terrifying image than a white (*Carchardodon carcharias*), with its conical-shaped snout, beady eyes, and serrated, triangular teeth. Descendants of prehistoric creatures, whites have been sensationalized by movies such as *Jaws,* or perhaps it's the realization that you are potential prey like the appealing harbor seal that puts you on the defense. Whatever it is, white sharks in particular trigger an irrational fear in many surfers. In his book *Caught Inside: A Surfer's Year on the California Coast,* Daniel Duane describes this neurosis as a state of "sharkiness."

White sharks grow as long as twenty feet, weigh up to 4,600 pounds, and can travel at seventy knots. Shark skeletons are composed of cartilage, rather than bone, making them hyperflexible: These sea monsters can whip around suddenly and bite prey behind them with their powerful jaws. Another strange trait of sharks is that they don't have the air bladders that help other fish float, so they sink if they stop swimming, a trait they have turned into an advantage. Without the air bladder, they can swim vertically, attacking their primary food source, pinnipeds, from below.

Sharks can see as well as humans, but they also identify prey in other ways with their seven sensory modules. For example, they have an acute sense of smell and electroreceptors that allow them to find prey. A surfer lying on his or her board can attract the fish sometimes mistakenly called "great white sharks."

The greatest population of whites can be found in South Africa, but more attacks on humans have occurred in California. A 150-mile swath from Monterey Bay to the Farallon Islands west of San Francisco to Tomales Bay to the north is known by the unappetizing name the **Red Triangle**. When considering the thousands of surfers, swimmers, sea kayakers, and divers who frequent the waters there, its not surprising these beautiful creatures cross paths with humans.

Surfers at these and other cold-water breaks have been attacked with some regularity. According to the Shark Research Committee run by co-founder Ralph S. Collier, nine unprovoked attacks were confirmed along North America's Pacific Coast in 2007. The figure equaled the previous Pacific Coast record set in 2004. The victims included two swimmers, one kayaker, one paddle boarder, and five surfers. The

DO'S AND DON'TS OF SURFING IN SHARKY WATERS

- Never enter the ocean alone.
- Don't surf at night. White sharks have daily feeding patterns and special crystalline cells like mirrors that enhance their night vision.
- Listen to your inner voice. Collier found that shark attack victims frequently said they had an eerie feeling just before getting bitten. If you are feeling spooked, paddle in immediately.
- Get three feet of surgical tubing and practice making tourniquets. Rig the tubing to your wetsuit with a Velcro strap in case you or someone else in the water is attacked. Some fatalities result from the victim bleeding to death.

Some tips for avoiding a shark attack:

- Stay away from areas known to be frequented by sharks. Tomales Bay and Año Nuevo are two locations that often report shark sightings, there are others.

- Stay in or near the kelp — there has never been a shark attack on a human in a kelp bed.

- There is safety in numbers. Most human-shark interactions happen when humans are few in number and isolated.

- If you see a shark while you're in the water — DON'T PANIC. Rapid flight will attract the shark. Remain calm and slowly work your way toward safety.

- If you are attacked by a great white shark, fight back. Counter attack has been effective in several shark attacks.

- Be aware of seasonal shark activity. In this region, sharks are most active in the fall, between August and November.

Adapted from "For Safer Ocean Enjoyment" by Dan Miller

Shark attack is one of surfers' biggest fears, as this beach sign attests, though few fatalities occur.

Sitting in the lineup, surfers are joined by California brown pelicans.

committee also reported that of the thirty-seven documented attacks along the Pacific Coast since 2000, surfers comprised 81 percent of the victims. Collier's book Shark Attacks of the Twentieth Century: From the Pacific Coast of North America has documented every known incident. Collier has discovered some important threads in the hundreds of attacks he has studied.

A majority of the attacks occurred in August, September, and October. Attacks recur in the same spots at the same time of year, such as river mouths when steelhead salmon are spawning. The salmon attract bigger fish, which in turn brings the pinnipeds, such as seals and sea lions. The white sharks couldn't ask for a more delicious setting. Silt from the river mouths creates sandbars with classically rolling waves, which have great appeal to surfers, but that happens to be in the middle of nature's smorgasbord, according to Collier. There are also repeated attacks at south-facing beaches in southern California when grunion spawn, as juvenile white sharks feast on the grunion.

It has often been thought that whites hit humans in a case of mistaken identity. Experts such as Collier reject this as myth. They say that sharks don't mistakenly bite us because they can make out shapes and see color. Whites can distinguish humans, with four dangling appendages, from a solid brown-skinned harbor seal. Another myth: Sharks are attracted to blood. A few years ago, a scientist put the theory to test by using every fluid manufactured by the human body. The sharks responded only to fluids from the stomach. If human blood were a stimulant, sharks would tear into a human after drawing blood, but that's not how attacks occur.

It's impossible to guarantee safety in the ocean. However, considering that millions enjoy the beaches during summer months, shark attacks are indeed rare. Humans, in fact, pose a far greater risk to sharks because of environmental degradation and overfishing. Yet, if you're a cold-water surfer along the Pacific Coast, you probably know someone who has experienced the horror of a shark attack.

The Three Types of Shark Attacks

- *Predatory attack.* An attack for the purpose of eating prey. The victim can get tossed four or five feet in the air from the impact. Whites also strike their prey with multiple bites.
- *Investigatory attack.* Sharks can be in-quisitive and carefully grasp a subject for a few seconds before letting go.
- *Displacement attack.* Sharks are territorial, like many predators. They will strike at something they perceive as a threat to their food supply or themselves. Surfing in shark-riddled waters means you're invading their territory, and they might not like that.

First Aid for Shark Bites

1. Treat the patient immediately on site.
2. Stop the bleeding immediately by applying direct pressure above or on the wound. If bleeding cannot be controlled by a pressure bandage, a tourniquet or leg rope may be tied tightly above the wound to block blood flow.
3. Keep the victim calm.
4. Seek immediate medical attention.

JELLYFISH

Jellyfish generally aren't a serious threat to surfers outside of parts of Australia. Although it's rare to find them in the surf zone, the gelatinous creatures do appear in places such as California, Florida, Hawaii, Texas, and Mexico. Getting stung by these marine invertebrates can result in discomfort and mild pain. Most are harmless, unless you have an allergic reaction.

Two species found in surfing paradises in Australia and Hawaii, however, present far greater risks. One is the bluebottle, also known as Portuguese man-of-war, which appears regularly along the Florida coastline, too. The bluebottles can be identified by their transparent, bluebell shape and long tentacles that carry thousands of stinging cells. Their sting is said to be three times as powerful as other jellyfish, but in most cases it's not fatal. Medical literature offers differing opinions about whether to apply vinegar when stung by blueys, although it now is generally accepted that it be avoided.

Another jellyfish species is one of the deadliest creatures in the sea: the box jellyfish, whose sting has been described as akin to being put into boiling oil. These pale blue creatures float into tropical north Queensland above Cairns in Australia, where beaches are lined with dispensers of vinegar for a life-saving application immediately after a sting. Enzymes from vinegar break down the venom. Immediate action must be taken if stung as some victims die within minutes of being hit. Others go into shock and drown.

Because of the scream-out-loud pain caused by the bluebottles and box jellyfish, many folk remedies have been used to neutralize the sting. A few of these are alcohol, ammonia, baking soda, meat tenderizer, unripe papaya, and urine. Although some swear by the curative powers of these substances, no conclusive studies substantiate their effectiveness. In some cases, these substances might cause more harm than good, so it's best to follow basic medical instructions when hit.

First Aid for a Bluebottle Sting

1. Use sea water to flush the tentacles from the skin.
2. Hot water is better than ice packs for managing pain from these stings, according to a 2006 Australian study.

Use water as hot as the victim can tolerate to make hot compresses.
3. Use a dry cold compress for pain relief if hot water is unavailable.
4. Don't rub the area even though it itches.
5. If the victim appears to go into shock, obtain immediate medical care.

First Aid for a Box Jellyfish Sting

1. Inactivate the nematocysts, or stinging cells, by flushing the affected area with vinegar. Leave the vinegar in place for thirty minutes.
2. Remove the stings while wearing protective gloves.
3. Use a dry cold compress for pain relief.
4. Obtain immediate medical attention.
5. Perform cardiopulmonary resuscitation (CPR) if the victim goes into cardiac arrest, which is a common symptom.
6. Don't rub the affected area.

BLUE-RINGED OCTOPUS

This creature is another delight from Down Under, home of eighteen of the world's twenty most poisonous snakes, as well as deadly spiders, sharks, and creepy saltwater crocodiles. These golf-ball-size octopuses are lethal, and they tend to hide in rock pools in the Great Barrier Reef. An attack is rare because they aren't aggressive. When a victim is bitten, he or she often doesn't realize it because the bite is not painful, but the octopus's venom contains a poison that can paralyze a victim within three minutes.

No antidote to the poison is known. The prescribed treatment is heart massage and artificial respiration. The poison usually wears off in twenty-four hours without leaving any side effects.

First Aid for a Blue-Ringed Octopus Bite

1. Use a pressure immobilization bandage in order to slow the spread of the poison.
2. If the victim has trouble breathing, perform mouth-to-mouth resuscitation.
3. Obtain immediate medical attention.

STINGRAY

Stingrays entered the public's consciousness in 2006 when Steve Irwin, aka the Crocodile Hunter, was fatally stung while taping a TV show off Australia's Great Barrier Reef. Irwin was killed when the ray's barb pierced his chest. Although the incident heightened fears of stingrays, the death was an extreme example of the dangers of these bottom dwellers. These rays aren't aggressive, although they will attack when provoked. Surfers in La Jolla, California, and at other warm-water beach breaks, have been zapped when accidentally stepping on a ray that is buried in the sand. These flattened-bodied fish have a long barb with a stinger that injects a toxin. Getting stung is painful and will result in bleeding.

First Aid for a Stingray Sting

1. Rinse the wound with fresh- or saltwater.
2. Carefully remove any remnants of the barb with tweezers, then scrub and rinse thoroughly.
3. Press on the area to stop bleeding.
4. Flush the area in water as hot as the victim can tolerate.
5. If the wound becomes infected, or if the victim feels unwell after an attack, obtain immediate medical assistance.

SEA SNAKES

Sea snakes are toxic creatures that pose a threat, albeit a slight one, in the tropics. Although more venomous than their slithery brethren on land, sea snakes steer clear of humans and rarely bite, even when provoked (though this isn't a license to bother one if you see it in the water). The deadly poison is not released in a majority of sea snake bites, thankfully, but you never know.

Sea snakes are found in Australia, Hawaii, and Indonesia in popular surfing locales. The venom takes about thirty minutes to affect a human, and the victim will then begin to feel stiff and achy. If untreated, the symptoms can progress to paralysis. It's important to get the victim to a hospital or emergency room as quickly as possible. As with many other snake bites, the victim should remain as still and calm as possible.

BARRACUDA

With their jagged teeth and streamlined bodies, barracudas are another fear-inducing creature of the sea, but they don't generally bother humans. Barracuda attacks have occurred, however, in Florida and Hawaii, especially with divers. California barracudas are smaller and, according to the Monterey Bay Aquarium staff, have never attacked anyone. The danger from a barracuda attack lies in bleeding to death. Barracuda teeth can cut through wetsuits and sever arteries. On land you can stop the bleeding by pressing down on the wound, but in the water you probably will need a tourniquet, such as a surfboard leash, to help stop the bleeding. Even if the bite is minor, you might need stitches.

STONEFISH

Considered the world's most venomous fish, the stonefish lives on reef bottoms camouflaged as rocks in tropical regions of the Pacific and Indian Oceans. It's yet another killer residing in the Great Barrier Reef of Australia. The stonefish has thirteen venomous spines it uses as protection from predators such as bottom-feeding sharks and rays. Unlucky humans get hit when they accidentally step on the fish or mistake it for a rock. The pain is said to be excruciating and can last for many hours. An incident can lead to temporary paralysis and shock and, in rare cases, death. Deep penetration of the multiple spines needs immediate medical attention and an injection of antivenin.

MORAY EEL

Eels are found in subtropical and tropical waters and look like long worms, but they have strong, sharp teeth that can inflict serious wounds. They usually don't attack unless provoked, so most surfers never have to worry unless they somehow accidentally fall or step on one. Moray eels often live in small holes or crevices in rocky areas.

SEA URCHINS

Sea urchins can be found in tide pools and shallow reefs, and in some cases their razor-sharp needles can puncture skin and produce a painful wound. If you accidentally step on an urchin, immediately remove the spines because some contain venom. The first step recommended is to submerge the afflicted area in hot water, which helps reduce the pain. Then carefully pick out the spines, which are fragile and can easily be crushed if you're too aggressive. Once the spines break off, they are more difficult to remove. You will probably see discoloration for the first two days because urchins leach an inky dye. If the discoloration persists, it could mean you failed to remove all the spines. See a physician for better treatment.

CORAL REEFS

Most waves at tropical islands break over coral reefs. While these reefs can produce extraordinary surf, they also present unusual hazards because corals are living organisms with a calcified shell. Surfers have been trapped by jagged coral branches and held under. More common are serious cuts and abrasions that burn and sting. Some corals are home to insects that can lead to nasty infections or poisoning that require immediate attention.

A SHARK'S TALE

Brent Laucher immediately regretted his decision to enter the water at the mouth of the Klamath River in Del Norte County, California, south of the Oregon border. His girlfriend had warned him against surfing one of the most shark-ridden spots on the Pacific Coast of North America. But Laucher allowed a stranger to talk him into surfing with him that foggy September day in 1998. It didn't take long for Laucher, twenty-eight at the time, to understand that the guy wanted someone in the water with him just to reduce the chances of being attacked. After forty-five minutes, Laucher decided to head to shore. He caught what he hoped was his last wave, but it broke quickly and spit him back into the **lineup**. He nervously paddled past the other fellow to wait for a good wave to take in.

Brent Laucher of Santa Cruz, California, survived a white shark attack while surfing mouth of the Klamath River near the Oregon border.

The wind suddenly shifted. Then three dark shapes moved toward him. As they got closer he identified them as sea lions. The first flew past Laucher without the slightest hesitation. Then the second. And the third. Instinctively, Laucher put his legs and arms on his board a moment before he felt the blow: "An intense hit like it went straight through me." Laucher was flung from the board and had the wind knocked out of him. Then he saw a flash of silvery white—the markings of a white shark. When he surfaced seconds later, he saw the shark mauling his board "like a dog ripping into it." He saw blood everywhere.

Suddenly the shark snapped out of its frenzy. The eye muscles dropped. The jagged teeth receded into the mouth. And Laucher found himself eye to eye with the creature. Then it dove at him. The shark, estimated to be a fifteen-foot juvenile, submerged with its tail slapping inches past Laucher. In semi-shock, the surfer grabbed his ripped board and paddled furiously toward shore as seals darted nearby. Laucher didn't check his body until he stood on the beach. Only then did he realize that he wasn't hurt. All the blood he had seen had come from the shark's gum, which was bleeding from gnawing on shards of fiberglass.

Laucher now has a greater appreciation for following his instincts. As he puts it, his internal bell rang loudly not to go out at a place he calls "a buffet table for sharks. They eat things, and I was on the menu for the day." As spooked as he was, Laucher surfed the Humboldt jetty the next day and hasn't stopped since.

First Aid for Coral Cuts

1. Scrub the wound with soap and water, and then flush it with freshwater.
2. Remove all coral splinters by rinsing or with tweezers.
3. If the cut stings, rinse it with vinegar or rubbing alcohol.
4. Flush the cut with a solution of equal parts hydrogen peroxide and water, and then rinse with freshwater.
5. Rinse the wound daily and apply an over-the-counter antibiotic ointment, such as Bacitracin, three or so times daily.
6. If the wound is infected, you might need more aggressive treatment from a physician who can prescribe a strong oral antibiotic or corticosteroids.

STINGING SEAWEED

Stinging seaweed, also known as stinging limu, is a blue-green marine organism that can be found in tide pools and deeper water in Hawaii, on the island of Okinawa in Japan, and in Queensland, Australia. Experts say most stings occur during the summer months when the plant drifts into swimming areas. The limu can cause a burning, blistering pain within twenty-four hours of contact. Although no antidote exists for a sting from this seaweed, it is generally more of an annoyance than a serious danger. Marine safety experts offer the following basic treatment tips.

First Aid for Exposure to Stinging Seaweed

1. Wash the skin and swimming suit with soap and water.
2. If suffering from itching, use Benadryl or an anti-itch hydrocortisone ointment.
3. For more severe symptoms, you might need to be treated with antibiotics or steroids.

CHAPTER 4

*A surfer pauses to meditate in the morning sun
before entering the surf.*

Fitness, Safety, and Etiquette

FITNESS FOR SURFING

Most serious surfers throughout the ages have been super fit. The old-timers needed bulk and strength just to lug hundred-pound-plus boards to the beach. They also relied on their physical prowess, as well as water-safety skills, because they put themselves in harm's way without a network of lifeguards keeping a watchful eye on the places where they surfed. These hearty souls helped formulate the backbone of surfing by providing the groundwork needed to be a waterman/waterwoman, including an unwritten code of conduct that hasn't gone out of style. They took pride in their physical abilities, which seemed to develop naturally over time by practicing their sport.

For the most part, they kept in shape by surfing, as it helps improve cardiovascular capacity and activates long-dormant muscles, including those on the back of the arms and in the lower back, calves, and abdomen. Beginners used to endure the pain of developing these muscles by slowly increasing strength as they learned to paddle and stand up. Many still ascribe to this tried-and-true method of increasing surfing fitness. But there's a more efficient way today, with personal trainers, self-help books, and twenty-four-hour gyms. You have many options for physically preparing yourself for surfing.

SWIMMING

The best way to start conditioning is by learning to swim correctly just as the original surfers who were expert swimmers did. In fact, swimming is not a step that can be bypassed as it's an essential skill for anyone venturing into an ocean. In addition, the stronger the swimmer you are, the more likely it is that you will advance quickly as a surfer. Thus, swimming should be incorporated into training at every level. But remember that being competent in a pool doesn't guarantee that you're ready for a steady diet of fast-moving ocean currents.

If you are serious about learning to surf and already swim well, consider taking the American Red Cross Water Safety Instructor Course. It offers instruction in the basics of water safety that ultimately could save someone's life, and its swimming requirements are an excellent benchmark by which to measure whether you are prepared to tackle big waves.

Most communities offer nominally priced recreational swimming lessons at public pools, where you can work on mastering your freestyle techniques. Competence in freestyle swimming will help you handle your surfboard better and swim more confidently and safely when you lose your board. You also should become comfortable with the backstroke because sometimes you must rest on your back amid rough currents.

Generally, swimming properly involves little adjustments of the body that take practice to master. An instructor can help teach good habits.

OPEN-WATER SWIMMING

While lap swimming provides the best opportunity to learn proper techniques, you also should swim in the ocean against strong currents because the more you know about the fickleness of waves and swells, the more adept you will be at riding them. After gaining confidence in the pool, try swimming at the beach where you plan to learn to surf. If it's a cold-water locale, wear a wetsuit to get used to your new environment with the gear you will wear for surfing.

Swimming in the ocean is different from swimming in a pool, so take it easy at first. When starting out, practice near shore on calm days. In the ocean, you might need to adjust your stroke a bit by

TIPS FOR BASIC FREESTYLE SWIMMING

Kick: Rhythmic kicking helps keep the body balanced in the water as your legs serve as propellers. You want to make little flutter kicks that save energy and keep you afloat. Some suggest kicking from the hips instead of from the legs. Others say keep your toes pointed.

Head: In the pool, your head should be in the water, facing down at the black lane line instead of out of the water to one side or the other. When breathing, you should rotate your body by shifting your hips while keeping the head down. If you move your head with your body, you will over-rotate and swim inefficiently.

Arms: A good freestyle stroke includes carving big S shapes with the right arm and backward S shapes with the left. Pull your hands past your hips to get the full benefit of each stroke. When you pull hard in the water, you get the most acceleration. Then extend your bent arm up in the air and as far out in front of you as you can for the next stroke.

Hands: Cup your hands, and knife them through the water at about eye level.

Breathing: Develop a regular pattern, such as two strokes and a breath on one side, two strokes and a breath on the other. Most people suggest rotating breathing from side to side while keeping the ear of the opposite side submerged.

rotating more side to side than maintaining the streamlined, balanced position you use in a pool. In the ocean you're usually not cutting through a still body of water. With wind and waves slapping at you, you need to find an energy-efficient method of gliding. By practicing in the ocean you will begin to feel how the undulating sea moves. And while ocean swimming builds your fitness, it also prepares you for paddling a surfboard.

GENERAL FITNESS FOR BEGINNERS

Surfing is an aerobic activity, so almost any exercise that increases cardiovascular fitness will enhance your surfing fitness. Endurance sports such as running and cycling are good cross-training programs.

Some surfers prefer running in sand, and quite a few enjoy mountain biking in nearby hills when the waves are **flat**. Mountain biking, cross-country skiing, and downhill skiing are good activities if you have access to snow and mountains.

The Importance of Stretching

The sun is out and the waves are four to five feet of perfection. You don't want to waste time getting to the lineup, but like any athlete you must warm up and stretch before practicing your event. Most physical trainers say a good fifteen-minute warm-up is enough to get you going.

Before racing across the sand and leaping into the water, take time to stretch at the start of every surf session. Stretching is important for many reasons, but foremost is preventing injury and muscle strain. You want to keep your body as limber as possible when participating in something that requires flexibility. The world's best surfers often are naturally flexible and contort their bodies instinctively to the variations of the waves, but even a wiry person should stretch first. Those who are stiffer can improve their surfing capability by incorporating simple stretches into their daily routine.

A stretching regimen should be included in any lap-swimming program. Some of those basic stretches also can be done on the beach. Many fitness experts say simple exercises on the beach that get your blood flowing are just as important as stretching. (They also suggest more prolonged yoga-type stretches to do after surfing to help in recovery and relaxation.) For help developing a routine that works for you, or to obtain more detailed instructions, consult a fitness trainer who surfs. For starters, though, find something that works and stick with it. Don't just rush into the surf—no matter how enticing that might be.

Some Basic Stretches

Do all of the following stretches slowly and smoothly, while maintaining control.

Arm stretching is part of the preparation to surf.

Coaching is helpful in learning the best form for stretching your shoulders.

Practicing knee bends on the sand

Using a surfboard to stretch legs and hamstring muscles

Arms: Make small circles with your arms, continually increasing the arc. Make big circles simultaneously with both arms. Then rotate the arms separately, remaining always mindful of moving slowly and consistently.

Shoulders: After loosening your arms, touch your left shoulder with your right arm by reaching behind your back. Now switch to the left arm, right shoulder.

Neck: Rotate your head to loosen your neck muscles. After a few rotations, reverse direction.

Back: Lie **prone** on the sand, and push your shoulders up while keeping your lower back stiff. This will help stretch the lower back muscles that you will feel while paddling.

Thighs: Spread your legs apart. In one smooth motion, lean with your hips to the right, then to the left.

Knees: There are many exercises to stretch the tendons and muscles around the knee; described here are leg lifts, the ilitotibial band stretch, and sitting knee bends. *Leg lift:* While lying on the beach, lift your leg four inches off the ground and keep it stiff. Hold the position for five seconds. Repeat at least 15 times. *Ilitotibial band stretch:* Cross the right leg over the left leg while placing the left hand on the right shoulder. Bend down and try to touch the toes with the right hand. Hold the position for at least 20 seconds. Reverse leg positions and repeat. *Sitting knee bend:* Bring the knee as close to the chest as is comfortable while sitting on the sand with the legs outstretched. Bring the leg toward the chest by gently pulling from the ankle. Hold the position for about 10 seconds, and then switch knees. Repeat five times.

Hamstrings: Bend forward at the waist and, smoothly, try to touch your toes.

ADVANCED TRAINING

You should incorporate some form of training regimen into each day, even if you're a recreational rider or just starting out. Surfing uses most of the body's muscles, especially when practiced at a high level. Many surfers say nothing gets you in shape for the sport like surfing itself does. There's something to be said for that philosophy. Spending hours in the water while chasing waves by paddling really is one of the best approaches, especially at the start. But once you get more serious about your surfing, you may want to adopt serious dryland programs tailored to surfing, which focus on a combination of power, strength, agility, and endurance. The big names, such as Kelly Slater, train like professional athletes in other sports to prepare for the punishment their bodies take in the ocean. Their structured workout programs develop and maintain endurance, core (the torso) muscle strength, balance, and flexibility.

Endurance

Before entering the water, you must have the stamina to handle the thrashing you'll take in the surf. This is especially important for beginners to understand. As you advance in skill you also must improve your endurance.

Surfer wipes out at Pleasure Point surf break in Santa Cruz, California. © Patrick Tehan

Clearing storm at Huntington Beach Pier in Huntington Beach, California. © Patrick Tehan

Grant Baker rides a wave in the finals in the 2006 Mavericks Surf Contest off Half Moon Bay, California, Tuesday, February 7, 2006. © Patrick Tehan/The San Jose Mercury News

A surfer takes on a wave at Steamer Lane surf break in Santa Cruz, California. © Patrick Tehan

Lombok, Indonesia. © Felipe Oliveira/Dreamstime.com

Bells Beach, Australia. © Kaan Calder/Dreamstime.com

Surfer mom Gretchen Ray and daughter, Sahara, share a moment at Capitola surf break in Capitola, California. © Patrick Tehan

Russell Smith gets airborne while competing in the 2006 Mavericks Surf Contest off Half Moon Bay, California, Tuesday, February 7, 2006. © Patrick Tehan/The San Jose Mercury News

Sierra Partridge catches a wave at Steamer Lane near the Lighthouse in Santa Cruz, California, Monday, January 15, 2007. © Patrick Tehan/The San Jose Mercury News

With the Long Beach skyline as a backdrop a surfer finds a wave on a flat day at Seal Beach Pier surf break in Seal Beach, California.
© Patrick Tehan

A shortboarder getting ready for a off the lip in Hawaii's clear water. © Kaz Sano/Dreamstime.com

Surfing Steamer Lane surf break in Santa Cruz, California. © Patrick Tehan

Cardiovascular programs are divided into two categories: aerobic and anaerobic. *Aerobic* means "with oxygen," *anaerobic* means "without oxygen." Aerobic exercises increase the capacity to carry oxygen throughout the body. The more oxygen it processes, the longer your body can function while being physically stressed. Anaerobic exercise involves short, intense activities that develop the muscles for quick bursts of energy, such as sprinting in track and field. Surfers benefit from both forms because endurance is necessary for paddling, and strength is necessary for going all out on a ride for three to five seconds.

Aerobic Training

Work on your aerobic capacity first. After a warm-up, you need only twenty or thirty minutes of medium to intense exercise to gain the benefits of an aerobic workout. Swimming is one of the best forms of aerobic workout, which is good for surfers because it's one of the primary exercises required for the sport. For those who enjoy cross-training, running and cycling also build endurance. Mountain biking is particularly beneficial because of the lung-burning aerobic workout you get while pedaling uphill, in addition to the strength and balance skills needed to navigate steep, narrow descents. Pedaling downhill on a mountain bike teaches you body awareness, a concept also known as *weight displacement*. Those skills transfer to the surfboard, where you are constantly changing your position to remain in proper balance.

Anaerobic Training

Anaerobic exercises include repetitions of weight-bearing drills or any quick burst of physical activity such as sprints or jumping rope. The exercise can't last long because of the buildup of lactic acid that contributes to muscle fatigue. You want to increase your lactic acid threshold so that your muscles don't go limp after the first explosive ride. You don't need to practice power weight lifting to build big muscles, but you want to stress your muscles much the way they will be when surfing.

Improving Core Muscle Strength

Consider building a program that works on the muscles connected to the center of gravity. Like a tree, you want to have a solid trunk. Create a daily program that develops the muscles of the back, hips, shoulders, chest, and abdomen and includes a warm-up, stretching, and a warm-down.

Surfing calls upon the body's core muscles to perform a variety of tasks. For example, upper-body strength is needed to perform the rapid movement of a **pop-up**. Most common upper body workouts in the gym, such as curls or bench or chest presses will suffice. These exercises will help with paddling, although you also should work your triceps.

Many surfers recommend using a balance (stability) ball to enhance your workouts. The ball can help you focus on the core muscles, thereby helping to prevent injury.

TRAINING TIPS FROM A BIG-WAVE PRO

As a child, Jenny Useldinger traveled the globe with her parents who surfed New Zealand, Indonesia, and other exotic spots. She followed their surfing footsteps but took it to the extreme: Useldinger is one of the few women to tackle monster waves. While living at Sunset Beach on Oahu's North Shore, she has carved a niche by traveling the world as a professional big-wave surfer. It takes a special mentality to ride the behemoths, as well as pinpointed physical preparation. Useldinger incorporates swimming and gym workouts and a few exercises designed for big-wave surfing.

LAP SWIMMING

Useldinger's workouts last 45 minutes: 15 minutes of warm-ups, 15 minutes of underwater laps, and 15 minutes of breathing exercises. After warming up, she holds her breath underwater for three lengths or longer. Then Useldinger

Big-wave surfer Jenny Useldinger incorporates a serious exercise regimen to complement her surfing. (Photo by Alexis Pasquariello)

works on breathing techniques with frog kicks. She rhythmically exhales when her knees come to her chest and inhales when kicking out. She finishes by swimming a length underwater to test her lung capacity with an accelerated heart rate. Useldinger then brings the heart rate down while underwater by staying calm. It's a way to learn to relax when being held down in big surf.

STRENGTH TRAINING

The idea is to work every part of the body. A gym session includes the following:

1. 30 minutes on a Stairmaster for a cardiovascular workout
2. Abdominal machine: 100 left, 100 right, 100 upper abdomen, and 100 leg kicks
3. Side Dip Twists: 20 left, 20 right with no weights; repeat with 5-pound weight; repeat with 10-pound weight; repeat with no weights
4. 100 back lifts over balance ball

5. 200 leg-up ball swivels
6. 10 chin-ups
7. 30 left, 30 right inner-thigh leg pulls with 20-pound tension
8. 5 left, 5 right outer-thigh leg pulls with 20-pound tension

FLEXIBILITY

Useldinger practices Bikram yoga, also known as "hot yoga," an intense form of stretching usually involving twenty-six postures and different breathing exercises practiced in hot, humid conditions. Useldinger likes the controlled stretch that puts her body into intense positions. "You're pushing yourself to the edge every time you paddle out," she says. "Anything you can do that resembles that kind of event will help your mental state."

OCEAN TRAINING

After losing her equilibrium while performing a duck dive in Hawaii, Useldinger began doing underwater dolphin spins to teach her body how to react in dangerous situations:

1. Perform a handstand on the ocean floor and start spinning.
2. Rotate with your hips.
3. Spin yourself to the point of dizziness.
4. Make sure you have a partner watching in case you black out.

BALANCE EXERCISES

Useldinger employs skateboarding to help build confidence about her balance. The activity trains the body to react to, and become accustomed to, motion. It also increases agility and muscle responses similar to those employed in surfing.

OVERCOMING FEAR

A fear of heights isn't conducive to big-wave surfing, so Useldinger has forced herself to face uncomfortable situations. With skateboarding, she must push off a cement ledge the way she would drop into a vertical 25-foot wave. In 2007, she dealt with her acrophobia by leaping off 20-plus-foot Jump Rock at Waimea Bay. Now when she does it, Useldinger imagines herself dropping into a big wave instead of **freefalling** into oblivion.

Some surfers use skateboarding as a way to improve their balance and body awareness.

A Few Basic Exercises to Increase Core Strength

Squats: Repetitions with weights can improve your reaction time for pop-ups. Squats can be executed from the floor using free weights or on a balance ball.

Push-ups: This exercise builds the strength to push off a board. Repetitions of basic push-ups are fine, though many trainers suggest using a balance ball. You can either place your hands on the ball and your feet on the floor or vice versa.

Bench press: While lying on a bench, a balance ball, or the floor, push weights above your chest.

Back extensions: Building your back muscles helps prevent injury while surfing. Lie face down with your hands behind your back and lift your upper body up a few inches for ten to twenty repetitions.

Lunges: While standing with barbells, step forward but keep your upper body straight. You want your forward knee to come to a ninety-degree angle. Step back and try it with the other leg.

Balance and Flexibility

Surfing is a sport of subtle body adjustments in reaction to an ever-changing, unpredictable wave peeling across the ocean's surface. To squeeze the most power out of the wave, you must continually move your feet and body in a delicate balancing act. The slightest misjudgment can result in a fall. You want to maintain stability in an unstable environment— **dynamic balance**—which requires core strength, coordination, and a low center of gravity. (It comes more naturally to shorter individuals.) Perhaps that explains why most of the world's leading surfing pros are shorter than six feet.

Flexibility is another aspect of balance. Those who start surfing as youngsters naturally enjoy a great amount of flexibility. Aging surfers must work to keep their joints and muscles as limber as possible to absorb the intense physical stress surfing entails. The better surfer you become, the more you need flexibility. Some waves require awkward-looking crouches that twist the body like a pretzel—some observers have called surfing "yoga on the water"—and the best surfers instinctively fold themselves into those positions. Obviously, the more you develop your flexibility, the more likely you will be to prevent injury.

Balance Aids

The Indo Board and similar products that simulate surfing in the home are being lauded as exercise tools by some users. Basically, these aids are skimboards on rollers, designed to help develop balance.

The SurfBall, another device, was invented by Brett Lickle while he was recuperating from reparative surgery to both knees, which he had damaged during a bad wipeout at Maui's **Jaws**. Lickle attached a board to a partially deflated ball that swivels around and forces you to work the muscles needed for surfing. To work it properly, you must get into a low crouch, grab the rails, and use good body positioning habits.

Some surfers stand or crouch on stability balls to practice balance. If any of these products, or others, helps improve balance

Surfers can improve balance at home with the help of a stability ball.

they are worth trying. Learning to surf is, in part, about developing balance, although some suggest you're either born with that ability or not.

Many manufacturers make claims about how their creations can dramatically improve balance and muscles. As with almost everything involving training or diet, opinions vary greatly on what works best. This book does not endorse any gear. *Bottom line:* You must adopt a program that is right for you.

The Indo Board helps surfers practice balance and positioning on land. (Photo courtesy of Hunter Joslin)

Inventor Brett Lickle demonstrates how his SurfBall can help surfers practice positioning and balance. (Photo courtesy of Brett Lickle)

LEARNING TO SURF SAFELY

Beginning surfers must master basic safety skills and first aid to prepare for emergencies. I was reminded of that one windless summer day in 1973, at the popular surfing spot called K55 just south of Ensenada, Mexico. My surfing was disrupted by a Mexican crying out no more than fifty yards from the lineup, where beautiful green lines danced across the reefs. He had drifted to sea without the strength to withstand the pounding surf that dragged him down. When I approached on my board, he lunged at me: A panicked swimmer often will pull the rescuer under with him. I calmed him, then gave him my board. He rested until his breathing normalized. Using the incoming waves, I kick-paddled him into the breakers as the board bounded toward shore. After a half-hour struggle, we made it.

Professional lifeguards supervise many popular breaks, but that shouldn't be a license to enter the ocean without basic water safety skills. A day does not go by without somebody getting into trouble. Sometimes you will find yourself at a remote break where help is hours away, and it will then be up to you to save a life. Tim Harvey, a veteran California state lifeguard and surfer for almost four decades, says that you should never assume a lifeguard sees someone in trouble; you must always be prepared to take immediate action to save a victim.

SAFETY BASICS

You must have a strong command of the ocean before tiptoeing into the surf. You must know the location of potential hazards, such as side currents (often referred to as rip tides), how to identify open channels (spots where the waves don't break, allowing a natural entry and escape passage to the lineup), and how to monitor the **duration** of wave sets (the elapsed time and number of waves that break during a given period). By monitoring the wave sets before surfing, you will know if the swell has lulls that will provide you with safe entrance or exit.

Even the world's greatest surfers are humbled by the ocean's power. Brett Lickle, one of the first to ride the giant waves at the famed outer reef of Jaws, almost died making a rescue of big-wave celebrity Laird Hamilton in December 2007.

The surfers were well prepared with every safety precaution imaginable, including radios and personal watercraft, yet they found themselves in a harrowing situation during a tow-in surfing session. Lickle was driving his high-powered personal watercraft (PWC) through the surf to fetch Hamilton when Hamilton fell on a particularly big **set**. Lickle quickly grabbed the surfer but couldn't get out of the **impact zone** before the next wave crashed. The big wave chased them, pushing Hamilton's wayward board with it. The wave knocked the men from the PWC, and the board's aluminum fins sliced Lickle's calf to his ankle. Five more big breakers held the surfers under until Lickle thought he might drown.

Fortunately, Hamilton found him in the surf and applied a tourniquet by tearing off his wetsuit and tying the sleeve around the wound. Hamilton retrieved the PWC, radioed for help, and eventually reached the safety of shore. Lickle, who needed fifty-six surgical staples to close the wound, credits Hamilton's emergency response with saving his life. He says every surfer should learn CPR and basic first aid when they start. "Once it goes wrong, you realize how small you are in this big world," he said.

RIP CURRENTS

Most surfers will never see the likes of Jaws at thirty feet, much less a hundred. They may however, encounter plenty of other dangerous conditions wherever they surf. One of the most common dangers is strong side currents, often called **rips** or rip tides. The phenomenon has nothing to do with tidal fluctuations, which are influenced by the gravitational pull of the moon and sun. Instead, the condition can be found when wave after incoming wave pushes onrushing water to the beach. That water must eventually return to sea, so it must find a way back out. If the incoming surf is too strong, it can't recede into it. So it goes around where there is less resistance. As a result, the currents rush out in a semicircular direction. You must swim parallel with the current until you are in still water, then head toward shore. Swimmers caught in a rip get in trouble by trying to swim directly to shore. As they swim in, they are actually pushed back out. The currents usually are stronger

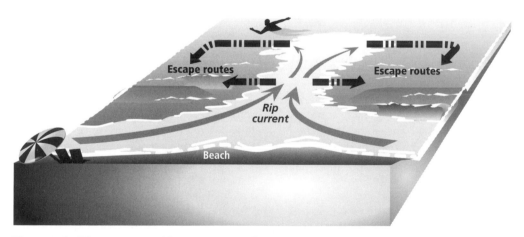

Rip currents. *Rips can create side currents as wide as 50 yards across. Swimmers caught in a rip current should swim parallel to shore until they've exited the outgoing current. Never try to swim against a rip.*

than the proficient swimmer. Rip currents become deadly when a swimmer is exhausted by fighting it and drowns.

Basic Safety Tips

1. *Know the break's intricacies before attempting to surf it.* Each surf spot has certain physical characteristics that make it special. You are best served by studying each place's traits before surfing there. Learn as much as you can from observation. Greater knowledge will come from months of surfing the place. You will begin to see where the waves break in different tides. This will help you know how to handle yourself when in the lineup. Also, always observe landmarks, be aware of your surroundings, and plan an alternate exit route before entering the water.

2. *Don't panic.* It wastes energy and can leave you disoriented. Most people drown because they panicked and became so fatigued that they had no strength left to get to shore. If you see someone panicking, try to calm them with a soothing voice. Always approach a drowning victim with caution. Don't let anyone lunge at you because that could endanger your life.

3. *Work with the currents instead of trying to fight them.* Use the waves as much as possible to bodysurf to shore. If caught in a rip, swim parallel to shore instead of directly against the current. You will soon discover that you are out of the rip and can safely swim to shore at full strength.

4. *If tired, rest by floating on your back or treading water.* It's easy to float in saltwater, so take your time until you're ready to swim again. This will allow you to relax and make better decisions when in difficult situations.

SURFING HEALTH HAZARDS

Surfing is considered to be an extreme sport, particularly for those who challenge twenty-, thirty-, and even fifty-foot swells. But most surfers don't face life-and-death situations even while riding **overhead** waves. A 2006 study of surfing injuries found risk increases for those challenging waves such as the notorious Pipeline in Hawaii. The study reached some other obvious conclusions: The injury rate more than doubles when surfing in large waves compared to smaller ones, and falling on a sandy bottom is better than one covered with reefs or rocks.

The author of the study, Andrew Nathanson, an emergency medicine physician and clinical professor at Brown University School of Medicine, also conducted a 1999 survey of 1,348 surfers. In his first study, he found that 66 percent of all injuries result from contact with a surfboard. About half of those result from being hit by one's own board. Recreational surfers reported lacerations and contusions as the most common injuries. Most of these injuries—cuts, strains, and sprains—are treated with conventional medicine.

MORE SERIOUS MEDICAL CONDITIONS

Surfers also are susceptible to issues beyond cuts, bruises, and sprains. According to literature provided by the Surfer's Medical Association, four maladies are prevalent: **surfer's ear**, hypothermia, muscle cramps, and skin cancer. (*Note:* All medical information here is general. Consult a licensed physician when experiencing specific conditions.)

Surfer's Ear

Cold water, wind, and saltwater have combined to become the surfer's enemy. The elements often lead to surfer's ear, or exostosis. The condition occurs when bone growth closes off the back of the ear canal. While painless, it can trap water and wax and lead to serious complications, including hearing loss. The condition should not be confused with swimmer's ear, an inflammation and infection of the inner ear usually caused by prolonged moisture. Surfers in tropical climates are more susceptible to swimmer's ear, but they also can contract exostosis because they are exposed to the elements for long periods.

The first symptoms of surfer's ear often are poor drainage and a ringing inside the ear. Some victims feel a sensation of being plugged up all the time. Improper drainage can lead to infections. If not treated, the bony growth can close off the canal, requiring surgery. Many physicians encourage preventative measures to protect the ear, such as silicone ear plugs or neoprene hoods to keep the inner ear dry. Earplugs are tricky because you want something comfortable

that won't affect your hearing and balance in the water. (Dr. Nathanson said no one has undertaken a peer-reviewed study showing the efficacy of earplugs.) The Surfer's Medical Association recommends coating the inner ear with olive oil before surfing and then drying the canal afterward by dabbing rubbing alcohol inside the ear.

Hypothermia

The use of wetsuits has turned surfing into a year-round sport and opened coastlines from England to South America to surfers. Even as wetsuits improve, however, surfers must understand the basics of hypothermia, a condition in which the body temperature drops below normal. The normal core body temperature is 98.6 degrees Fahrenheit (37 degrees Celsius). Scientists have found that cold water decreases body heat at least twenty times faster than air does. A drop of seven degrees Fahrenheit can lead to internal organs shutting down. In other words, hypothermia can be fatal.

It's important to know the telltale signs. Shivering is one early symptom of hypothermia. If you begin shivering uncontrollably, you should get out of the water and change into dry clothes, then immediately try to warm up with hot liquids or a warm shower. If you don't, you might start to lose coordination and mental capacity and not realize where you are.

When the core body temperature drops dangerously low, the victim stops shivering. Anyone who notices this change in a fellow surfer should get the victim out of the water immediately. In such critical situations, it's

Apply sunscreen before hitting the waves.

important to get the victim to a warm place, drape him or her in blankets or towels, and have the victim drink warm liquids. If the victim fails to respond, call 911 to seek immediate medical help.

Important: It is *not* safe to put a victim in advanced stages of hypothermia into hot water.

Muscle Cramps

A cramp is a painful tightening of the muscle, and a cramping muscle is the bane of every athlete. Surfers' calves are most susceptible to cramping, which is more prevalent in colder climates. Some causes of cramping are dehydration, salt or mineral deficiencies, muscle strains or overexertion, and a too-tight wetsuit that restricts blood flow. When you experience cramping, it's best to exit the water to stretch and gently massage cramping muscles.

It also is important to be hydrated. Your favorite sports drink should suffice. Nutritionists also suggest eating fruits, vegetables, and grains—the kind of vitamin and mineral-rich diet recommended for any athlete. Surfers can also learn from runners and others who fight off cramping with electrolyte gels.

Skin Cancer

The American Cancer Society reports that more than a million Americans are diagnosed annually with non-melanoma skin cancers, most of which are curable. But 60,000 Americans are diagnosed annually with melanoma, which is sometimes fatal, according to the group's 2007 statistics. Surfers are highly susceptible to the damage of ultraviolet rays because they are exposed to the elements for long periods of time. Not only are they in the water, but they often hang out at their favorite beaches all day.

The American Cancer Society advises limiting exposure to the sun between 10:00 AM and 4:00 PM. For many surfers, that works fine as the waves are better at dawn and dusk since there is less chance of wind at those hours. But those surfing midday are advised to wear sunscreen with a sun protection factor (SPF) of at least 15. Also, it's best to use a waterproof product and reapply it often. Other preventive measures include wearing a hat on the beach or, if surfing a small break in the tropics, while in the water. Rash guards and neoprene vests also protect the skin when surfing in warm climates. Finally, it is important to wear a good pair of sunglasses to protect the eyes from ultraviolet damage.

Fair-skinned surfers should monitor changes in skin coloration and check with a physician at the first sign of change. The American Cancer Society (www.cancer.org) provides basic information. The American Academy of Dermatology (www.aad.org) also offers informative guidelines.

SURFING ETIQUETTE

The ever-increasing crowds at the best surf locales have transformed the sport from a genial enterprise into one with enough neurotic behavior to fill a psychiatrist's notebook. Surfing can be one of the most unwelcoming activities known to humankind, a contradiction to its Polynesian roots and the laid-back image promoted by Duke Kahanamoku. By the 1960s, surfers had become so protective of their local spots that they employed guerrilla campaigns to discourage outsiders: They slashed car tires, hurled insults, and even started fistfights. This type of churlishness has been branded as "localism," and almost every surfer has experienced it.

A RISE IN LOCALISM

The tipping point for surf aggression came in 2000 when Nat Young, a legendary Australian surfer nicknamed "The Animal," suffered a gruesome beating after an argument over a wave at his home break in New South Wales. Young, who has accepted responsibility for initiating the argument, was hospitalized with two broken eye sockets, two broken cheekbones, and smashed sinuses. The experience profoundly changed Young, fifty-two years old at the time. He wrote a book about surf rage, saying he wanted to expose a slice of the sport that had existed for a long time.

About the same time as Young's assault, Chris Brewster, San Diego's former chief lifeguard, mounted a campaign to get his state legislature to adopt the California Open Waves Act. A draft of the law stated that no person "regardless of residence, lineage, social status, or other reason may lawfully claim the right to a wave . . . along the California coastline." Although the law failed to pass, the effort highlighted the serious effect of localism.

OVERCROWDING

The ocean has become an overcrowded playground with a finite number of waves to go around. By the early 2000s, surfing had become a $7.5 billion industry. The sport has attracted millions of participants and shows no signs of leveling off. The growth is underscored by the hundreds of surf schools that discharge the relatively uninitiated to the beaches each week. When adding in baby boomers on longboards, Boogie boarders, kayak surfers, and the like, surfing hardly resembles the idyllic activity romanticized

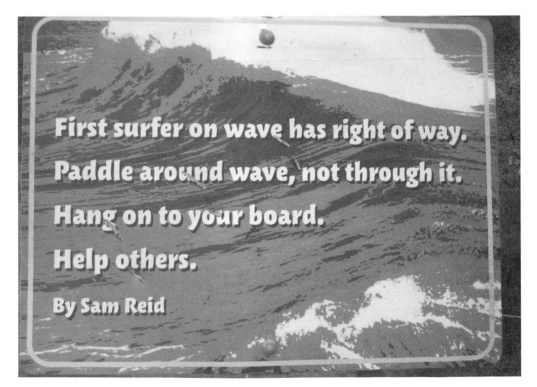

First surfer on wave has right of way.
Paddle around wave, not through it.
Hang on to your board.
Help others.

By Sam Reid

The basic rules of the break are posted for surfers at Santa Cruz's famous surfing locale, Steamer Lane.

by authors Mark Twain and Jack London.

When Hawaiians surfed thousands of years ago, they generally rode straight into the shore. The practice allowed for many to share the same gentle wave, but once surfboards got fins and surfers began planing across the wave's face, the presence of more than one person per wave diminished the experience. For that reason, regulars at any given locale frown on newcomers, particularly a crowd of novices. Today, getting into the lineup at a popular surf break can feel like driving in a bustling metropolis.

KEEPING THE PEACE

The following etiquette tips can help you maintain peace in the water:

- ■ *Right-of-way.* The person up first or closest to the breaking curl has priority. When someone has the right-of-way, do not take off in front of him or her. That's called **dropping in**, and it's also known as snaking, cutting off, or shoulder hopping. It can be dangerous, especially if a beginner drops in on top of another surfer. Experienced surfers often break this rule, but they shouldn't. Never take off in front of another, even if it's the only wave you'll get for the day.
- ■ *Kicking or hurling your board.* Don't kick your board at someone who drops in on you. It could result in a debilitating injury. Furthermore, don't hurl your board in the air when falling. For your protection, and that of others, always be mindful of the danger of a flying board.
- ■ *Be humble and courteous.* Apologize if you make a mistake, and control your temper when another person does something wrong. If you cause someone to fall or end up in a collision, make sure the other person is okay.
- ■ *Get into the lineup with care.* Whenever possible, paddle around the break to reach the lineup. Look for channels to the side of the break where it's easier to paddle in. Avoid paddling through the break and causing a logjam.
- ■ *Whenever possible, do not paddle in front of a surfer riding a wave.* When surfers are caught during a set of waves, those riding the waves have the right-of-way. Steer clear of the wave's face when an oncoming surfer approaches. Instead, paddle behind the surfer, which means going into the rushing white water. Getting pushed backward by powerful surf is better than getting smashed by a fast-moving board. Besides, it's good karma not to impede another's wave.
- ■ *Avoid letting go of the board when faced with an oncoming wave.* The board becomes a projectile that could hit another surfer or swimmer. **Duck diving** or **turning turtle** are the best ways to keep hold of a board (see chapter 5).
- ■ *If paddling for a wave with another surfer, state whether you're going left or right so that the wave can be shared.* Communicate clearly and without malice.

By following these principles, you can help reduce interpersonal tensions in the water and make the experience more like the one that Duke Kahanamoku enjoyed sharing with the world.

A MOM TAKES ACTION

Maggie Hood calls it "Too-Close Day." On January 2 of each year, she takes her daughter Marissa to her favorite restaurant to celebrate her well-being. "I could be caring for an invalid right now," Hood told me.

On January 2, 2004, Marissa Hood had paddled to a local break in Ventura, California, to surf and research a middle-school science project about how waves are shaped. She ended up floating face down in the water for a few minutes after getting smacked by another surfer's board. She was hauled to shore by other surfers before being taken to a hospital. She only remembered being underwater. "I opened my eyes and it was grayish, and it was really peaceful. 'Oh, I'm underwater and I should get up,' but I couldn't move," Marissa recalled.

The Hoods say a man on a longboard deliberately ran down Marissa, thirteen years old at the time, as she paddled to the break. After the incident, Maggie Hood received calls from parents of others who had suffered similar fates while surfing. She realized that Marissa's experience was not an isolated one. It led the Ventura real estate broker to launch a one-woman campaign against reckless surfing. Hood founded the Surf Safety Alliance (www .groundswellsociety.org/surfsafetyalliance) to promote good manners. One letter found in a local internet chat room dedicated to surfing accused Marissa of being inexperienced. In essence, it was saying she got what she deserved. That incensed her mother. "Whether you're experienced or not, there will come a day when you're **caught inside**, and what? They're going to run you down and that's okay?" Hood asked. "No, it's never okay. You must not injure another surfer. There will be another wave. This whole mentality, 'It's my wave' is wrong. It's easy to say, 'She was in my way.' But you hit her. You almost killed her."

CHAPTER 5

A surfer rides a left-breaking wave while partially hidden by spray breaking against the rocky cliffs.

Surfing Technique

As a preteen, I used to spend late summer Sunday afternoons at the end of Broadway Street in the seaside village of Laguna Beach, California. My parents wanted to exchange the inland heat for a breath of salty air. I went for the waves. I rode a hard piece of yellow Styrofoam in the rough shorebreak at Main Beach. Such boards were the precursor to the Morey Boogie Boards, Tom Morey's ingenious invention that helped introduce millions to riding waves. The **foamies** were prehistoric in almost every aspect—stiff, fragile, and utterly unreliable as a vessel moving through water. But riding it on my belly taught me the basics of wave action.

Main Beach has a shallow sandbar offshore that makes surfing difficult because the waves **wall** up and crash near the beach. If the swell is up, it has fast-running rip currents and is dangerous for inexperienced swimmers. I didn't know any better. Back then there were no lifeguards and few

people around. Just me and my foamie. I reveled in the exhilarating rush of boiling white water hurling me toward shore. I got knocked around, but I eventually learned to work with nature's forces, to find that sweet spot on the board, and to navigate the board safely. Then one early fall day, as the waves gained momentum behind the power of hurricane swells from Baja California, a large breaker grabbed hold and flung me to the shallow bottom. When I regained my composure I discovered my foamie had been snapped in two, ending my first foray into the surf.

It takes time to become comfortable with the ocean, so don't expect much in the beginning. Muscle memory develops slowly, so it's important to cultivate it little by little. Treat initial forays into the surf with Zen-like calmness: Embrace the moment, even while the surf slaps you back to Omaha. Depending on one's natural instincts and body awareness, it can take months to get comfortable standing on a malleable moving object. Gradually, it will become easier and easier to navigate the forces.

No one, even those who suggest otherwise, has an infallible method of teaching surfing. And you won't find a secret passage that gets you to your goal of riding waves quicker than others. Use a mix of approaches: Learn with friends; find a mentor and surf school lessons; watch surf videos and read instructional books; learn to bodysurf or bodyboard as a precursor. Whatever approaches you use, some basic skill sets—lying, paddling and sitting on the board, and learning how to pop up and catch beginners' waves—apply universally and can be studied and practiced first on land and then in the sea. It's best to become skilled at each of these systematically before graduating to the next. In other words, it's a step-by-step process that builds on each skill. Ultimately, though, it's up to each individual to harvest the skills and

knowledge needed to ride waves through the long-established system of trial and error. Put simply, the more often you get in the water, the quicker you will gain the dexterity needed to surf.

LEARNING WITH FRIENDS

When encountering an environment as foreign as a surfing break, where locals often have a proprietary interest in discouraging new faces, it's nice to have someone along for support. It's also fun to commiserate with friends after a particularly aggravating outing. So find friends who are interested in learning, and develop your skills together.

A healthy amount of laughter is indispensable in carrying you through the most frustrating moments, of which there will be many as you learn to surf. All those grim-faced expert surfers with squinty eyes scanning the horizon need just such

A surfer executes a bottom turn on a small wave at a beach break. (Photo by Caitlyn Kenney)

a reminder sometimes. As individualistic as surfing is, it is also a social activity with shared memories that last forever. (When old surf buddies gather, they talk as if they were war vets about epic days.)

The buddy system also has practical applications. Although everyone has a fantasy of finding a secret break of their own, surfing can be dangerous, so it's always advisable to surf with someone else in the water. A friend or two can come to your rescue in a worst-case scenario. More likely, friends will push each other to do better, to abate fears of big swells and those sharp-toothed creatures lurking underneath the surface.

BEFORE SURFING

Know what the ocean feels like before attempting to stand on a board. Two of the best ways to gain this knowledge are body-surfing and bodyboarding. By practicing these activities, you will gain the wave sense needed to catch waves and be safe. You will begin to understand how waves break and where to catch them, how to dive underneath, and how to find the lineup.

BODYSURFING

Find a beach break where you can learn to bodysurf. Start on a day when the waves are small, and practice in a swimming zone where lifeguards are stationed. Stand with your back to the wave just below the curl.

Then dive with the wave as it crashes. At first, you will go **over the falls**, which means you'll cascade down the wall of water. Eventually, try to stiffen your body into a planing surface and skim diagonally across the wave's face with one arm outstretched. Use swim fins to power into bigger waves. Once you master the skill, bodysurfing feels like flying.

A good way to gain wave knowledge is to start riding bodyboards, such as the Boogie Board.

A note of caution: In rare instances, you can injure your spinal cord by conking your head or straining your neck during a steep fall into a shallow sandbar. When a wave batters you, make sure your arms protect your head. Also, don't fight the turbulence when submerged. Hold your breath and stay at the bottom as long as you can until the worst of it passes. Try to remain relaxed at all times.

BODYBOARDING

Another activity that teaches you about waves is bodyboarding. Californian Tom Morey made it popular in the 1970s with his Boogie Board, a durable, rectangular slab of flexible Styrofoam designed for supreme maneuverability on the wave. The premise with bodyboarding is similar to bodysurfing, but instead of using your stiffened body to skim across the wave's face, you lie on a board. **Bodyboards** teach you how to ride waves by manipulating the body weight from side to side. One intrinsically learns the feel of the ocean, such as the way currents move and where waves break. You also learn the mechanics of paddling while lying on your stomach. Expert bodyboarders do **360s**, **bottom turns**, **smack the lip**, and other tricks that translate to surfing. But more than anything, it's a safe and fun way to learn to surf before trying to stand up.

PRACTICING ON THE SAND

Most surf lessons begin on the sand with an instructor advising students how to practice the basics, such as lying on the board, paddling, and standing up. While no amount of land drills can replicate the experience in the water, it's advisable to take these steps seriously when beginning. Once upon a time, surfers lugged their boards directly into the surf and eventually figured it out. But those who practice on the beach first will have a leg up because they will have learned some basic skills in a controlled environment.

You usually don't learn every skill on land before getting into the water. Instead you learn one skill, such as paddling, and then try it out in the sea. After gaining some comfort with paddling, you should return to the beach to learn the proper drills for standing. None of this is something that you can accomplish in one day or one surf lesson. If your goal is to stand up in the white water near shore, then sure, you can probably achieve that quickly. But if you want to learn to surf properly, take it slowly and follow the steps described. You will get to the lineup and catch your first wave sooner than you think.

LYING ON THE BOARD

The first point to learn is to lie prone on the board. A big part of mastering this skill is having a beginner board. You want to make sure you have a blunt-nosed and wide longboard, which offers stability when in the prone position. When using a fiberglass board, make sure it's correctly waxed; otherwise you will have difficulty lying on a slippery deck. Once the board is waxed, you must discover your "sweet spot" on the board: where you're balanced just right when paddling. You want to figure out how

Instructor Matt Cole, owner of University of Surfing, shows his class how to do a pop-up.

to paddle fluidly, and the way you lie on the board helps to accomplish that. If you're too far forward, the board's nose will pearl, or sink. You might slip off the front, or it will be difficult to remain aboard when bashed by the frothy foam. When lying too far back, the nose will point up, resulting in the tail dipping into the ocean and the board going nowhere. A more embarrassing episode also could result. Because you are too far back your board could shoot out from under you in what's called the **torpedo effect**. Being perched just right

will make it easier to paddle over the ocean's bumpy surface and get you to the break with the least amount of exertion.

No amount of guesswork can replace getting in the water and finding the sweet spot by feel. Those lucky enough to have a mentor or instructor join them in the water will get better advice on how to lie correctly. Many factors go into finding an efficient position. Height, weight, and board length are the most important. As a result, surfers must adjust their positions every time they switch boards.

TIPS ON POSITIONING

1. Disperse your body weight from the center of the board so that the nose is just off the water.
2. Keep your legs stretched out instead of dangling off the side.
3. Raise your feet just off the tail.

Apply a fresh coat of wax before trying your new skills on the water.

Find the correct spot to lie on your board.

The board will pearl if you lie or stand too far forward.

After practicing on land, try out what you've learned in waist-deep water near shore just to get a feel of lying on the board in the water. Let the surf knock you off the board. Then lie on the board for ten minutes and experiment by shifting positions to see where you feel most balanced. After that, it's time to head back to the beach to learn to paddle.

PADDLING ON THE SAND

Beginners rarely spend enough time learning to paddle because they are too eager to try to stand up, but here's a secret: The more proficient a paddler you are, the better chance you have of catching waves. The sea's uneven motion can feel unmanageable for the first few months, and most beginning paddlers try to compensate for

Paddling technique

THE BASICS OF PADDLING

1. It's best to use the pull-and-reach technique. This is accomplished when one arm is pulling in the water while the other is reaching, like paddling a canoe. Also known as the Australian crawl, it provides the most forward movement of any stroke.
2. Take full, rhythmic strokes. Quick, shallow strokes are not as efficient in propelling the board.
3. Pull hard—and with your whole body.
4. Cup your hands like you would for the freestyle swim stroke.
5. Pull harder to one side when turning the board.
6. Bring your legs together, making sure your feet are pointed down. (Some surfers bend their knees slightly so the feet rise out of the water a few inches.)
7. To slow the board down while paddling, lift your head and shoulders off the deck while keeping your legs straight. To gain speed, keep your body flat on the board, with your chin inches from the deck.

that by spreading their legs wide. However, you should lie on the board with your back slightly arched, hands cupped, and legs straight. Take long, smooth strokes from the nose, pushing away the sand on the side. You want to get a feel for your muscle movements before facing bouncy seas.

PRACTICING IN THE WATER

It's beneficial to take the board out on a flat, **glassy** day and paddle around the ocean to get used to stroking correctly without becoming panic-stricken by incoming swells. Not only will it be a great workout, but it will allow you to safely begin to get the feel for the balance needed to paddle effectively. While this sounds simple enough, be prepared for a frustrating struggle because you won't be as stable as you were on the beach.

To get started, find a convenient beach that you can park nearby. There is no reason to lug the board a long way to the shore. Also, stay away from more challenging breaks with rocky cliffs or jagged ocean floors. You don't want intimidating physical barriers getting in the way.

Once you find the right beach, enter the ocean. When walking out, turn the board sideway, tuck it under your arm, and grip the rail with your hand. Keep the board away from your face because even a small wave packs a wallop. If the ocean is calm, walk the board toward the break by laying it on the water and guiding it with one hand while heading out. (Point the nose toward the horizon when going out; point it toward the beach when coming in. This will help protect you from losing the board and getting hit by it.) While walking your board to where you want to begin paddling, you might be confronted by a small ripple in the water. Push down on the board's tail, and the board will pop over it.

Once you're in waist-deep water, practice paddling. Apply all the lessons you learned on sand. First, situate yourself on the board correctly—you can tell by the way you are balanced. Then practice long, fluid strokes and see how the board feels underneath you. It should move forward. Work on balancing yourself so that your legs are straight and your feet are lifted above the tail. Focus on getting comfortable with the positioning.

After practicing on calm days, paddle into small swells to learn how to navigate them. If you're not sure whether conditions are safe, check the colored flags at lifeguard stands that designate surf levels. A **green flag** indicates small; a **yellow flag** warns of medium but risky levels; and a **red flag** indicates dangerous levels. It's always good to ask another surfer or lifeguard if you're not sure about the conditions. As a beginner, practice only in green-flag conditions. When heading out, you will likely encounter currents and wind waves strong enough to frustrate your efforts, so be patient and heed the following general rules.

Surfers walk their boards to the break in low tide, until the water is past their waists.

GENERAL RULES FOR PRACTICING IN THE WATER

- At first, work with the white water. Let the onrushing soup go underneath you by slightly submerging your board with a half push-up. Sure, you'll get pushed back, but the idea is to stay on top of the board and keep paddling against nature's forces.

- Paddle away from the wave's impact zone. When paddling up a wave's face, it's fairly easy to paddle over it as long as it's not about to curl. The concept is to paddle up the shoulder, then slide down the back side. If you're caught near the curl, you probably will be thrown to the trough, so always try to avoid the wave's crest.

PADDLING IN THE WATER

Always learn the ways of the ocean before you enter the water. Then set moderate goals, which means not worrying about standing up right away, whether that's your first day or week or month.

Never pay attention to what other surfers might think. In fact, the best days to practice are the windy ones when they won't be around. While strong winds create crumbling, or poor, surf, it's worth hitting the beach on a **blown-out** day. After all, you want to practice in the white water instead of a real wave, especially if you haven't graduated from bodyboarding.

Always study the waves before you enter the ocean. Watch for ten minutes to get a sense of where they are breaking. Find a landmark on the beach, and keep it in sight so you will always know your location: It will help you gauge if you're too far out or too close to shore or have drifted away from where you intended to be. Next, paddle out past the initial breaking white water. Get out far enough that you will have a long ride to shore in the white water.

It's easy to tell where the white water begins while observing from land. It's much more difficult once you're in the water and trying to paddle through the misty surf. Most beginners panic and turn around at the first blush of a roller snapping them. You almost need someone to pull you to the right spot so you know where to start at first.

Practice paddling out and riding the white water to shore on your belly. It helps develop good paddling skills and teaches tentative surfers to begin to harness the power of waves. Wait for a river of white water to flow toward shore. Before it reaches you, turn the board around to face the shore, jump on it, and make sure you are positioned correctly. Start to paddle toward shore until the foam hits you and you have the sensation of being lifted up a bit. When you feel the wave taking hold, grab the rails and enjoy the ride to the beach.

Try this over and over to get used to the sensation of being pulled along by the wave. As you become more comfortable, try angling your board one way or the other to begin the initial lessons related to weight and body control. Soon you will discover you can use the wave's energy to move the way you want. Once you have control of the forces and your board, try riding it in on your knees. Do this over and over until you gain a measure of confidence. The natural progression will be to stand up next.

STANDING UP

Once you are proficient on a board while lying down, it's time to practice good techniques for standing. As in finding the sweet spot for efficient paddling, it's important to discover the best place to stand on the deck. The first step is to figure out whether you are a **regular footer** or a **goofy footer**. These terms are part of surfing idiom. They signify which way a surfer naturally stands on a board, which is really no different from being right-handed or left-handed when hitting a tennis ball or baseball. A fun way to discover your natural tendency is to ride a skateboard. Which foot do you automatically put forward? If it's your left foot, then you are a regular footer, which means you will face the wave while riding toward the right. If your right foot is forward, you're a goofy footer. It's important to distinguish which you are because the movement to stand up starts with your front foot.

Sometimes it is better to try riding on your belly, then your knees, before standing up.

Practice in the sand to learn to stand correctly on a surfboard.

The proper stance usually begins in the center of the board, knees bent, legs spread just beyond the shoulders. The front arm should be thrust forward about chest high and pointing toward the board's nose whereas the back one should be bent and located just below the face. Think Ninja attack stance. Practicing this stance will save headaches later because it's the fundamental position of standing.

The Pop-up

For experts, standing comes naturally and quickly. Most don't even think about the action because their minds already are plotting the next three moves down the wave's face. But for beginners, the act of standing is all they can consider while floundering about on a shaky board. Watch expert surfers as they power into the waves: where they place their legs, how they push fluidly off the board. Make mental notes of surfers' popping up when watching surf videos. The more vivid the image you have created, the easier it will be to understand the mechanics. Basically, standing requires a quick, smooth push-up while sliding your front leg forward and ending in a crouched position. You rarely stand erect, except on longboards.

The Pop-up. *From the prone position quickly push off the deck of the surfboard with your hands and your back foot. At the same time bring your front foot forward to help push up; end up crouching in the center of the board with the legs spread a little wider than the shoulders.*

How to Do the Pop-up

1. Start on a flat part of the beach while lying on your board as if you were paddling.
2. From the prone position put your hands securely on the board's deck about 2 inches from the rails at chest level. Also make sure your feet are planted firmly.
3. Quickly push up while keeping your feet under your body and pushing with your hands and your back foot (right foot for regular footers, left for goofy footers).
4. As you push up bring your front foot forward to provide leverage in getting up.
5. You should find yourself crouching in the center of the board with your legs spread a little wider than your shoulders. The front leg should be centered between your hands.
6. Your feet should be turned sideways, planted on the board.

Rising from the Knee

When beginning, some find it easier to push up from their back knee. This is okay as long as it doesn't become habit. Here's

Starting on your belly, quickly pop up by pushing up on the board.

what you do: Instead of going right into the crouched position while sliding the front foot forward, use the strength of the back leg to push up, with the bent knee on the board. Keeping your hands on the rails, balance yourself by leaning back. Make sure to turn your body sideway as your front foot slides forward while the back leg holds you steady. Once the front leg is properly positioned, push up from the rear knee. Don't forget to wind up in the crouched position with your legs spread and feet pointing sideway.

Standing in White Water

For most people, the act of standing up while riding the white water comes naturally: At some point, you try to stand up on the moving board, but this simple act can be mastered more easily by following a system. If by now you are riding on your belly or knees for a good distance, you are ready to try standing.

A System for Standing Up on a Board

1. Turn your board toward shore and jump on it as the white water breaks.
2. While lying down, steady yourself by making sure you are balanced correctly.
3. Now practice the pop-up while moving by pushing up on the board and swinging your back foot next to your front knee.
4. While balancing the board with your hands, carefully rise from a low position. You don't need to stand up straight at first. Get used to riding the

wave a couple of times while almost on all fours, if necessary.

Sitting on the Board

You also must learn to sit properly on the board. It's a bit like sitting on a horse. It takes practice to feel comfortable sitting while waiting for the waves, but it's worth the effort. Mostly, surfers sit on their boards to monitor the horizon for the next set of waves. They can see farther than if they were lying on their boards, craning their necks. It also ensures that they remain close to the lineup instead of drifting with the currents. In breaks blessed with bobbing kelp forests, surfers sometimes tie a slithery band around their ankle to anchor themselves. That's difficult to do, though, from the prone position.

Sitting isn't as difficult as the pop-up, but some of the same techniques are used. While lying on the board, begin the push-up motion of the pop-up. The front of a short board should dip into the water slightly while you sit up. Pull the board forward through the legs, and then it should be straddled firmly. This movement will be awkward at first. The board might even slip through your legs as you fall backward, but your legs will help you stay balanced. If you lean too far either way, you might tip over. You will feel incompetent, but with practice it will become second nature. *A tip:* Scoot up slightly if you're sitting behind the board's center. The nose should be level with the water or just submerged.

As with paddling, it's best to learn to

Sitting on top of the board makes it easier to react when the sets arrive.

sit on the board in calm, shallow water. Eventually, however, it's essential to get used to sitting up underneath rolling waves or, in some cases, strong currents.

At first, most surfers keep their hands on the board for balance, but eventually they become comfortable enough to sit casually or to maneuver the board by paddling from the sitting position. They do this to outmaneuver others in the lineup so they can be in the prime position to catch a wave.

Paddling for a Wave

Once you have mastered sitting, it's time to learn how to paddle for a wave from the sitting position. Expert surfers easily turn their boards from the sitting position because sometimes they must react quickly to an oncoming wave to get into position to take off. It's a maneuver worth practicing in shallow water.

To begin, hold on to a rail with one hand and slightly lift the nose of the board out of the water by shifting your weight back. With the other hand back, begin to paddle by pushing water away from the board. The board will turn to the side you paddle.

When a set marches into the lineup, surfers experience a sense of urgency. Everyone jockeys for position to have the right-of-way. As a result, they waste no time in dropping into a prone position to paddle hard toward the breaking wave. You must learn to shift effortlessly from sitting to paddling. The slightest hesitation could mean losing position to take the wave.

How to Shift from Sitting to Paddling into a Wave

1. Lean back slightly, and push the water away from the board with one hand while pivoting toward the beach.
2. Scoot your body toward the board's tail to quickly get into the proper prone position.
3. Once balanced correctly while lying down, paddle to the wave.

CATCHING A WAVE

After spending enough time in the sea to understand its quirks, it's time to paddle to a small break to try to catch a wave. Before heading out, study the break, and make sure it's for beginners. Don't go where the experts are; you don't want to start on the most difficult break. A beginner's break has rolling waves without steep drops that crash onto shore. Avoid walled-up waves that break top to bottom, and look for broad, sandy beaches. Some of the best beginners' waves are found at

Old Man's at **San Onofre State Beach** (though it's often too crowded), Cowell's in Santa Cruz, and Waikiki in Honolulu. Ask a local surf shop employee to recommend the best place for novices. Even if it goes against your machismo spirit, make sure you are going to a beach that's appropriate for learning to surf.

Once you're ready, paddle into a wave near the breaking curl. More advanced surfers take off as close to the peak as possible because they want the steepest, fastest ride they can get. As a beginner, though, you want to take off on the gentler slope of the wave's shoulder.

Points to Consider When Catching a Wave

- Figure out whether the waves are right or left breaking. You want to begin where you ride front side; in other words, right breaking for regular footers and left breaking for goofy footers.
- Observe from shore to see where the waves curl, as well as where other surfers are catching them. What is the easiest way to get to the lineup? Figure this out ahead of time.
- Know what kind of beach you are surfing: sand, reef, point break? You want to surf sandy beach breaks when you're starting out.
- Stay out of other people's way.

Once you graduate past white water, you must learn some advance moves for paddling because larger waves create more intense situations. Two essential techniques are duck diving and turning turtle.

The duck dive. *Submerge the board's nose as the wave begins to curl. Take a deep breath and push the tail of the board to keep it level; point the board toward the surface and paddle once the wave has passed.*

The Duck Dive

The basics of the duck dive can be learned while bodysurfing. Stand waist deep in front of a **hollow**, breaking wave and dive underneath the impact zone. As the wave breaks, pop up behind it and—yes—breathe a sigh of relief.

Learning to duck dive is crucial, particularly for fast-breaking beach breaks but really for anywhere one encounters big curlers. Unfortunately, duck diving is an option only for those riding shortboards; it won't work with a longboard. The maneuver seems like something out of *Star Wars* because you must flow with nature's energy instead of trying to fight it. While it is often possible to paddle furiously up the face of a humongous wave and safely **punch through** the **lip**, at other times you will be caught so far out of position that you will be crunched unless you and your board dive deep.

How to Perform a Duck Dive

- As the wave begins to curl, submerge the board's nose by pushing hard on the rails. You want to perform a half push-up to let the wave flow between you and your board.
- As the wave crashes over you, most of the board must be underwater.
- Take a deep breath, and make sure your knee or back foot is pushing on the tail of the board so it's level underwater.
- Go as deep as possible directly under the turbulence, or impact zone.
- Once the wave passes, which you will feel, point the board toward the surface and begin paddling again.

Turning Turtle

Another way to safely survive the surf is the technique of turning turtle. Whereas those who ride shortboards can use this or the duck dive method, longboarders must rely on turning turtle because their boards are far too big to fully submerge.

A turtle turn

How to Turn Turtle

■ Turn the board over with fins facing up, and pull the board hard toward you so you end up beneath it just before the wave breaks.

■ Hold on as tightly as possible, and brace for being pulled toward shore.

■ Once the wave crashes, flip the board over and begin paddling.

The Takeoff

The idea is to paddle into the wave, with your board's nose pointed toward shore, by building enough velocity to match the speed of the wave. Experienced surfers instantly know when they reach that point; although difficult to describe, it's a pas de deux with the wave, and it's all about timing. Surfers will paddle hard toward a peaking wave, stop, turn toward shore, take two or three solid strokes to catch it, and then smoothly pop up. Beginners often misjudge the timing by paddling too soon or too late. As the wave approaches, paddle toward the peak and make sure another surfer isn't farther back than you and trying for the same wave. Turn the surfboard toward shore and begin paddling, all the while checking over your shoulder to monitor the progress of the wave moving toward you. As the wave begins to pick you up slightly, point the board toward the direction you want to be heading, which will be right or left. At the moment the wave propels the board, ride it at an angle on your belly or knees the first few times to get a better feel of where to place your body.

It's important to get a good feel for the wave because, once you're on it, body placement will determine how successful the ride is. If the body is stationed correctly, the board should glide along the wave's green face until it dissolves into the foam. It's good to ride it all the way to the beach to get more comfortable on the board and to practice paddling back to the lineup. This is sufficient for the beginner. You simply want to practice catching the wave at the right time and quickly popping up at a slight angle. Then just glide along for as far as you can. The next steps, which involve much more intricate balancing and body placement, are covered later in this chapter.

LEARNING TO FALL

Learning how to safely fall is part of controlling your surfing. While a wipeout seems to be a spontaneous, uncontrolled action, adroit surfers almost always are aware when they're about to **eat it**. As a result, they react appropriately to protect themselves from bodily harm.

Even when you know the ocean's traits, such as the type of bottom where you're surfing, you must always be prepared for a fall. When surfacing after a fall, check for your board, oncoming surfers, and waves headed your way.

Matt Cole, owner of University of Surfing in Pacifica, California, has students practice sticking their arms over their heads and crossing their hands to form a V as if they were preparing to dive into a pool. That's because the biggest danger isn't sharks or drowning. It's getting banged by your own board.

One of the first good habits to develop is to put your hands out as soon as you begin falling, whether forward or backward. That way you can protect your head from cracking into a hard piece of fiberglass floating nearby. Once you've fallen, it's important to gauge where your board is. An easy way to do this is to pull your leash. If it's tugging your ankle after a wipeout, the board is a safe distance away. If there is no restraint, use caution when resurfacing, and do so with a hand above your head.

For sure, you are going to fall off the board the first hundred times you get to your feet, but practice falling while you're in the early stages of standing up. Once you feel comfortable standing in the white water, work on controlled falls off the back of your board.

Tips for Falling

- Take a deep breath as you fall because you are going to be submerged under water.
- Cover your head, or raise your arms to protect your head.
- Try to fall backward, but if you fall into a breaking wave, try to dive deep (like a duck dive) to allow the curl to pass over you.
- Don't dive headfirst into any water. You could hit the bottom and suffer a spinal cord injury.
- If you fall into turbulent swells, you may lose your sense of direction. Don't panic. Once the impact subsides, look around to see where you are before you head to the surface.

The basic skills presented in this chapter thus far are sufficient to get you on your way. If you are willing to take the time to really master each skill set, you will soon become a proficient surfer. As previously stated, the more you can get in the water to practice, the better you will become. It is equally important to emphasize that this process should be fun. Riding the white water should transport you to an idyllic childhood, flooding you with nostalgic feelings of being free and unfettered. The same goes with standing in the white water and then paddling to the break. As the level of difficulty of each skill set increases, you should find you're having more fun. Sure, a particularly hard wipeout is never what you'd call a pleasurable experience, but that's part of this game. Once you're up, you're bound to be brought down, but by now you are a bona fide surfer.

INTERMEDIATE SKILLS

These skills should be learned at the localities you're accustomed to surfing. There's no need to put you, or others, in harm's way because of bravado. You should be able to find enough variation to expand your ability near the places where you learned the basic moves.

Learning more difficult maneuvers comes naturally when imitating fellow surfers or trying out what you've seen in a video. Once you are comfortable enough in the lineup to ride medium-size waves, you should get an instinctive feel for the physics of board movement. Positioning the body correctly is fundamental to surfing well. By shifting your weight forward, the board will plane faster across the face. Pulling your weight back will slow it down. You must have supreme board control if you hope to graduate to the three fundamental turns—the bottom turn, the **cutback**, and the **reentry** or top turn.

Your stance is perhaps the most important element in the intermediate phase. Although no single model describes the perfect stance, keeping your knees bent and using your lower torso to balance yourself on the board are key. You must also switch your stance, depending on the wave or even a **section** of the wave. For example, if you're riding a long point break, you can generate speed by staying high in the wave's face and leaning slightly forward. If you want to carve a turn instead of jetting across the surface, you will have to reposition yourself on the board.

BASIC TURNS

The first maneuver to master after learning how to take off and angle down a wave's face is the bottom turn, perhaps the most essential surfing maneuver because it's the move that transfers energy from the drop to produce most of the other actions you will take. **Front-side** and **back-side** are the two types of bottom turns. The names refer to how you stand on the board. If you are a regular-foot surfer, you will ride front side—front facing the wave—on right breaks. If you're a goofy foot, you'll ride right-breaking waves with your back to the water.

The front-side turn is easier because you're facing the wave and have a full view of how it's breaking. Upon takeoff you often slide with great speed down the wave's face to the trough, only to rebound back to the top. The latter part of the maneuver is the bottom turn. When you reach the trough, or flat part of the wave, you perform a U-shaped turn back to the crest so you can continue riding the wave.

How to Make a Front-Side Bottom Turn

- After dropping down the face, crouch and lean into the wave with your head, hands, and feet facing the wave. Be careful not to lean too far and fall off the board.
- Place your trailing hand in the water to help get your body in the right position as you shift your weight on the board.

It takes advanced skills to challenge big swells.

A bottom turn is the most essential maneuver to learn once a surfer can stand up.

- Redistribute your weight onto the inner rail, the one closest to the wave's face.
- Maintain your balance. If you lean too much with your back foot, you could pop a fin and lose control of the board.
- As you ascend the wave, shift your weight to the back foot to slow down the board and prepare for your next move, which connects to the bottom turn.

How to Make a Back-Side Bottom Turn
- Upon descending to the bottom of the wave, crouch and lean back on your heels slightly, with your back to the wave.
- Look over your front shoulder to see what the wave is doing, but keep steering the board down the wave with the lower half of your body.
- Shift your weight to the inside rail by leaning your back into the wave. You should begin turning toward the crest.

THE CUTBACK
The cutback is a horseshoe-shaped turn that guides you from the shoulder back toward the wave's power source where it's curling.

You must learn to perform this maneuver if you want to prolong rides. If you get out too far in front of a wave, you will **stall**. Cutbacks now have many derivatives, but you should try to master the most fundamental one: a **roundhouse cutback**. The cutback is often a continuation of the bottom turn. You must execute the bottom turn correctly to set yourself up for the cutback.

How to Make a Front-Side Cutback

- Start at the wave's top, and essentially ride back-side along the wave's face.
- Lean on the outside rail with your heels.
- Look back at the oncoming wave while continuing to lean onto the rail that is biting into the face of the wave.
- Keep a low center of gravity as you reach the breaking wave.
- When hitting the foam, apply weight to the inside rail as you switch directions again.

How to Make a Back-Side Cutback

- To start, lean on your inside rail with the balls of your feet.
- As you make the first horseshoe turn, place your trailing hand in the water. You can then turn around your arm as if it were a ski pole.
- Watch your speed while heading back to the crest.
- When you hit the foam, switch to the outside rail by leaning on your heels. Making the second horseshoe turn can be difficult because you have ended up

with your back to the wave again. It's like making an S-turn. Practice the backside cutback in smaller surf until you are comfortable with it.

THE REENTRY

The reentry is a more detailed maneuver than the other turns. It's completed on steep, hard-breaking waves. The idea is to go up and down the face in rapid succession to remain close to the power source the entire time. After making a precision bottom turn, you will quickly elevate to the wave's lip. To perform a reentry, you will reverse the board's direction when you hit the lip. On a good reentry, the top third of your board will be pointed above the wave momentarily before it slides back down the face.

Quick, precise bottom turns and reentries are the stuff of experts. Intermediate surfers should focus on getting to the lip and back down without worrying about trying to make vertical turns. The reentry is important to master because it will help later on with expert maneuvers.

How to Make a Front-Side Reentry

- After performing the bottom turn, guide the board back toward the lip, just in front of the curl.
- Lean into the wave and rotate your hips while maintaining your balance with your legs and feet.
- As you hit the wave's lip, shift your weight to the outside rail. Make sure you put weight on your back foot in a fluid motion.

Surfers perform cutbacks at Steamer Lane in Santa Cruz, California, to return to the curl.

■ When the board is pointing out of the water, your shifted weight will force it back down the face. This is the flash point of the move, and it happens so quickly your board will suddenly reverse direction.

BACK-SIDE REENTRY

Once perfected, the back-side reentry is one of the more satisfying moves because of the control you have when **hitting the lip** from the back-side position. But it takes a bit of juggling to do it right. You have to twist your torso in one direction while the lower half of your body remains anchored to the board.

How to Make a Back-Side Reentry

■ Upon completion of the back-side bottom turn, twist your shoulders and head toward the top of the wave to see where you want to direct the board.

A surfer pulls off a back-side reentry.

- Gently shift your weight from the inside rail to the board's center to help stay balanced as you climb up the wave.
- Bend your knees and shift your weight to the back foot as you hit the lip.
- Once about a third of the nose is facing skyward, reverse directions by turning your torso toward the bottom. Your board should follow your lead and switch directions too.
- Push hard on the back foot so the board rapidly reverses position.
- Head down the wave's face while crouched.

TUBE RIDING

Although tube riding is for experts, thoughts of it enter the surfer's psyche soon after starting the sport. Surf magazines and videos bombard audiences with enticing images of surfers in barrels in sun-kissed locales such as Oahu's Pipeline, Bali, or Tahiti. The scene rarely changes: A turquoise-colored, almond-shaped cylinder splashes into a bursting, white cloud that obscures the deepest interior of the breaking curl. From this wide-angle vantage, the surfer's trailing hand can be seen dragging along the face, his eyes as intense as a prizefighter's.

On average, though, most surfers don't find waves with curling sections that make tube riding possible. Not only must the wave be hollow, but it has to have a well-shaped shoulder. Otherwise, you will get buried inside the curl and not make it out. While slow-motion action films show tube rides lasting for an eternity, they rarely are longer than three seconds.

To pull off a successful tube ride, you need catlike timing and a fearlessness about taking off late, sometimes behind the peak. Once on a wave, you must be aware of what is happening behind you to set up the ride. When you sense a fast-curling pocket closing in, stall your board by placing weight on the back foot. Submerging your tail will dramatically slow down the board. You will feel the presence of the wave about to break over you. It is usually best to stay high on the wave's face. Once you feel the wave cascade overhead you will lose sight of the beach. Time might slow down, like in the movies. Drag your trailing hand in the wave's face to give yourself a sense of balance, and slow the board for control. You'll probably need to crouch, tilting forward slightly to get the board moving again. Stay calm and let nature's beautiful force push you into daylight. If you're too deep, or the wave lacks a nice shoulder, you'll probably get swallowed by the curl. Any time you think you're falling while in a tube, try to drop off the back of your board and dive deep underneath the turbulence. You don't want to get caught in an out-of-control position where the lip flings you backward into the trough. An uncontrolled fall could lead to serious injury.

CHAPTER 6

Challenging big swells, such as winter waves, takes advanced skills.

Taking the Next Steps

A strange feeling overcame me just before the hard-charging wave slammed into the rocky reef on an island off Baja California, Mexico. It felt as if I were being sucked backward with electromagnetic force. In rapid-fire frames, I saw rocks and land whiz past and then plop. I hit the water so hard my contact lenses popped out. This was the position I found myself in one winter's day in 1983 while charting new waves on the relatively unknown island of **Todos Santos**, ten nautical miles west of Ensenada.

Back then, before computer formulas were used to predict swells, a surf trip was as much about the surprise and excitement of finding waves as riding them. Once they advance past the beginner stage, surfers often come down with the travel bug as they want to exercise their newfound skill sets on bigger, faster, and more exotic waves. It's part adventure travel, part

rite of passage for budding surfers as they discover the power of maneuvers such as bottom turns, cutbacks, and off the lips. For southern California surfers, the hunt used to mean trips to Baja or Hawaii. Australians and New Zealanders would head to Bali, Indonesia. Those forays often broadened worldviews and brought travelers closer to surfing's multinational culture of fashion, food, literature, and music.

Before venturing away from home, make sure you've mastered the basic and intermediate techniques outlined in chapter 5 so you'll have the ability to handle new and sometimes challenging surfing conditions.

We needed serious skills upon landing at Todos Santos because we arrived as one of the biggest winter swells of 1983 hit. That prodigious season was fueled by a dramatic **El Niño** condition, blessing the West Coast of the United States, as well as Hawaii, with some of the best surfing waves in history. While thousands enjoyed good surf along the mainland coast, we rode Todos Santos's XX-size offerings without crowds. At the time we surfed there, the desolate isle wasn't well known among surfers. It would gain celebrity status a few years later as a major stop for big-wave surfers.

The main break now known as Killers went off at thirty feet or higher. None of us dared paddle into the lineup at Killers; it can be daunting to surf a relatively unknown break that looks fierce. Besides, we found plenty of big, powerful waves at four other breaks on Todos Santos. By the time I lost my contacts on the final morning of the trip, I was ready to bid the island adieu. My arm muscles cried in pain. My thirst for waves was sated. Back in California we shook hands, promised to stay in touch, and had the look of kindred spirits. We knew we had experienced an epic surf trip.

SURF TRAVEL

Modern-day surfing embodies the freedom of travel. Unlike drifters, though, surfers travel with a sense of purpose. They go where the waves are—or to rocky shores that offer the promise of surf. A big part of the sport's magic once involved chancing upon great waves. Some old-timers still practice the wave hunt by packing their vans and heading north or south along the coast, but in the hurry-up society in which we exist today, who has time? Sean Collins, one of the world's leading wave forecasters, says the days of cruising up and down the coast looking for signs of a swell have passed. Collins and other forecasters provide surfers with what they need to know about where to go almost anywhere in the world.

For die-hard surfers short on free time, it's worth utilizing a reputable forecasting

A shoulder-high wave at Smokestacks in Huntington Beach, California

service to maximize your surfing holiday. The world has become so small it's now possible to monitor the waves in front of Greg Miller's Sandpiper Inn in Playa Hermosa, Costa Rica, with the surf cam found at his website, www.sandpiper.com. Not only can you track the swells, but you now can see what the waves actually look like at places such as Miller's.

PLACES TO GO

It has become much easier to reach some of the more exotic places as adventure travel has grown exponentially since the 1990s. Major surfing destinations now include Australia, Brazil, California, Costa Rica, Florida, France, Hawaii, Indonesia, Fiji, the Maldives, Mexico, New Zealand, the Philippines, Samoa, South Africa, Spain, and Tahiti. A segment of the travel industry now caters to surfers, including those at the beginning and intermediate levels. It's possible to take a two-week beginner's surf vacation in Costa Rica, Hawaii, and many other places. Luxury resorts are found near some breaks, a far cry from the days of surfers sleeping on the beach or in their vans and subsisting on convenience store donuts.

When traveling to new surf spots, expect the unexpected. Traveling to new places never turns out exactly the way it

A surfer flings off the top of a good-size wave.

SURF TRIP ESSENTIALS

- If planning to travel abroad, make sure your passport is current. You also might need a visa to enter all of the countries you are planning to visit. The U.S. Department of State website, www.travel.state.gov, lists country-by-country requirements for international travel.
- Depending where you're headed, you may need to bring a few boards for a variety of wave conditions and surf breaks. If you can take just one board, always bring your favorite.
- Use board bags and Bubble Wrap to pack your board because you don't want to land in paradise and discover your board has a bad gash from transport.
- Pack the following equipment:

  Extra fins (If you have removable fins, remove them before transporting the board. Keep the lock key in a safe spot because you'll need it to insert and remove the fins. Get a fin protector for nonremovable fins.)

  Extra surf leash

  Wetsuit, depending where you are visiting

  Booties, to protect your feet on coral reefs or cold water

  Plenty of wax and wax removal equipment, such as a plastic comb

  A ding repair kit

  Sunscreen

  Hats

  Rash guards

  Sunglasses

  Extra board shorts

  Lightweight long pants

  Sturdy shoes and sandals

  Beach towel

  Insect repellent

  Digital camera

  First-aid kit (This should include prescription medicines and anti-diarrhea medication. Check the Centers for Disease Control and Prevention [www.cdc.gov] for special items you'll need in the region of the world you are visiting.)

Use a board bag for protection when transporting your surfboard to the beach.

had been planned. Some of the experiences are memorable, others forgettable. The benefits often involve meeting new friends, sampling local cultures, and experiencing other elements that spur personal growth. The obstacles of surf travel usually involve facing hostile locals. California surfers, for example, might not receive a welcoming committee if they travel north of the Oregon border. Some spots, such as those in Humboldt and Del Norte Counties in northern California and Oahu in Hawaii, also are notorious for bad vibes. The best way to endear yourself to locals is to show respect and to surf at breaks within your ability level. You must research a new place before traveling there. By doing your homework, you will be better prepared to soothe over the difficulties inherent to travel.

FOREIGN TRAVEL

Traveling to some locales can include the added inconvenience of language barriers, parasites in drinking water, stinging bugs, and biting sea creatures. If you plan to visit a foreign country, see a travel medicine specialist to figure out what you need to protect yourself. You might need vaccines against hepatitis A, tetanus, malaria, and typhoid. If traveling to places where malaria is a problem, consider special mosquito netting for sleeping. Always try to learn a little bit about the country before landing there. Picking up a few basic phrases in the local language will make your trip much more satisfying. Always pack a good sense of humor.

WHEN TO GO

The art of surf travel includes spending time surfing, not sitting on the beach gazing at a flat, wide horizon while waiting for a swell. That's why online forecasters have grown in popularity. You also should know the primary surfing seasons. On the north shore of Oahu, for instance, the best waves arrive from October to March. The famous Pipeline will look like a lake in the summer months.

Countries in the Southern Hemisphere have seasons opposite those to the north. In other words, it will be winter in Australia, Brazil, and New Zealand during summer in North America. Tropical places, such as Costa Rica, have a dry (winter) and rainy (summer) season. Costa Rica provides an interesting model for much of Central America because it encompasses many of the region's traits and issues. Beyond knowing the seasons, it's important to know that you're usually dealing with the Pacific Ocean and the Caribbean Sea. On the Pacific side, the swells come during the summer, or wet, months. To the east, along the Caribbean coastline, it's often rainy year-round, and the surfing conditions follow the hurricane season that begins about June.

SURF CULTURE

Until the 1960s, surfing remained a niche activity that attracted little interest outside its bubble. Few noticed that the sport's practitioners had created a subculture that eventually would become a lifestyle embraced by

Surf art is displayed at the International Surfing Museum in downtown Huntington Beach, California.

millions. Surf culture began as an amalgamation of elements plucked from the beaches of Australia, California, and Hawaii.

The cultural roots are strongest in Hawaii, where the sport originated. With warm water and vibrant sun, Hawaiian surfers eschewed formal wear for short pants, floral shirts, and flip-flops. They also had a laid-back aura that has come to symbolize surfing—even if it's something of an embellishment. Colorful personalities adopted Hawaiian ukulele and slack-key guitar music as their own, and they spoke in a jargon that helped distinguish the cultural boundaries. Californians who went to the Islands for the big waves in the early 1950s returned under the spell of Hawaiian fashion, music, art, and speech patterns. Australians followed quickly. Now the cultural cross-pollination has expanded to include features of Brazilian, French, Indonesian, and other beach subcultures.

GOING MAINSTREAM

In the late 1950s, popular culture wasn't only about Elvis Presley and the new technology of television. Surfing began to gain some traction through grainy, amateurish surf films. Then the *Gidget* franchise debuted in 1959. The story of teenager Kathy Kohner spending a summer surfing at Malibu became fodder for a popular film adapted from a novel by Kohner's father. *Gidget,* so named by Malibu surfers as a blending of "girl" and "midget," introduced the beach's mystique to the public. Almost overnight the sport attracted millions, and that fueled the board-building industry. What had been a capricious lifestyle enjoyed by a handful became a way of life adopted by the masses. Hollywood saw an opportunity and pounced with films such as *Beach Blanket Bingo,* which exploited surf culture and turned it into something otherworldly.

Surf music followed with vibrato guitar instrumentals from Dick Dale and his Del-Tones and the Ventures, as well as pop song hits by the Beach Boys and Jan and Dean. Clothing manufacturers began mass producing the "surf look" of wide-stripe t shirts and swimming trunks. By the twenty-first century, the culture had been integrated into mainstream society to the point that surfing was being used to sell cars, clothes, and a sexy lifestyle. Little of this had anything to do with the unadulterated feeling of paddling into a glassy, fast-moving wave and angling down its face. And surfers found it difficult to maintain an outlaw image with the sport's business estimated to be more than $7.5 billion, a majority of that derived from the fashion industry.

SURF FASHION

Originally, surf fashion involved creating something practical to wear while surfing. Woolen tank-top suits popular in the 1920s were worn by pioneer surfers. In the 1940s, Los Angeles surfers bought old sailor suits and cut them off above the knees. But the surf trunk transformed into more than comfortable attire. It became a costume that emblematized a lifestyle. When the surfing boom hit in the 1960s, southern California companies began making trunks dedicated to surfers. Nancy and Walter Katin, who made canvas boat covers, manufactured trunks out of their Orange County offices. Dave Rocheln, another trunk maker, was inspired by the florid colors of Hawaii. In 1964 he introduced **Jams**: baggy, colorful swim trunks with a name that was derived from "pajamas." During this era the bikini also became popular, but surf clothiers hadn't yet realized the growth potential of marketing to women. By the late 1970s, entrepreneurial surfers had started their own companies, continuing to push designs to remain relevant to current fashion trends. Some of the big-name companies were Quiksilver, Gotcha, Instinct, and Maui and Sons. Often these trends started on the beaches, then moved inland to become popular with those who had never seen an

MY FIVE FAVORITE SURF SONGS
"Breakdown" (2005), Jack Johnson
"California Saga" (1973), The Beach Boys
"Crumple Car" (1968), Denny Aaberg and Phil Pritchard
"Pipeline Sequence" (1972), Honk
"Walk Don't Run" (1960), The Ventures

ocean, but surf wear still emphasized board shorts and t shirts.

Surfers wore simple clothes on shore: white Levis and Pendleton jackets in the 1960s; t shirts with favorite surf shop logos, straight-leg corduroys or blue jeans, and flannel shirts in the 1970s. In the 1980s, the apparel business was jolted by the influx of women surfers. As companies expanded, they began selling their brands in department-store chains, the most evident act of turning America into Surf Nation. Now it's really not about clothing surfers anymore. The brands sell the image of youth-oriented, healthy living. Outdoor companies market sunglasses, watches, shoes and sandals, shirts, and pants more than they do board shorts.

SURF MUSIC

The origins of surf music can be found in the chants of the *kahuna,* or Hawaiian priests. The music didn't take shape until the 1950s when filmmakers used instrumentals of the era for the soundtracks

Opposite: A guitar from a famous surf rock band of the 1960s is showcased at Huntington Beach's International Surfing Museum.

of their surfing documentaries. The genre, though, has mostly been associated with the sport's golden era of the early 1960s. Some say surf culture was cemented between 1960 and 1965. If so, music played a major role. The Ventures released their hit "Walk Don't Run" in 1960. Dick Dale, the "King of Surf Guitar," followed with "Let's Go Trippin'" in 1961. The Rendezvous Ballroom on the Balboa Peninsula in Newport Beach, California, became the center of the scene where the popular bands of the era played the surfer stomp, a twist on rockabilly and rhythm and blues. Author Leonard Lueras wrote in *Surfing: The Ultimate Pleasure* that instrumental groups surfaced "from every other suburban tract home garage." The Beach Boys and Jan and Dean spun simple tales about southern California surfing to further popularize the beach sound. Until the Beatles and the English invasion, surf music permeated America's youth culture.

Even though the genre of surf music referred to the innocent sounds of the early 1960s, surfers found commonality with current musical trends. In the 1970s, for example, Neil Young's "Cowgirls in the

Riding back-side on a big, right-breaking wave

Sand" provided the backdrop for a powerful sequence in a surf flick. One of the most memorable soundtracks of the era came from a Laguna Beach, California, group named Honk. The talented Orange County band created an up-tempo LP for the 1972 hit *Five Summer Stories* by Greg MacGillivray and Jim Freeman. Some of the instrumentals captured the mood of the post-hippie era and were perhaps more closely aligned with the generation than with surfing, but the sequences also encapsulated the spirit of the shortboard revolution. Performers such as Hawaiian surfer Jack Johnson have continued the tradition by creating music linked to surfing.

SURF MOVIES

The film industry has done as much as any medium to promulgate surf culture. Whether they're die-hard documentaries or embellished fictional accounts produced in Hollywood, surf movies have created and polished the stereotypes that remain part of the sport. Any discussion of surf filmography must be split into two categories: documentary style and commercial movies.

Bud Browne generally is credited with creating the surf film genre in the 1940s. The former schoolteacher really got going in the 1950s, producing at least one film a year from 1953 to 1963. As the sport became popular, a few other filmmakers joined Browne to develop a format that was heavy on surfing action in big waves, instrumental scores, and travelogue. Bruce Brown's *The Endless Summer,* released in 1966, perfected the formula that included a comedic narrative. Following tan, lean, and blond-haired Californians Mike Hyson and Robert August on a foray around the world, the film solidified widely held beliefs about the look and capriciousness of surfers. The movie not only epitomized surfing culture but became the sport's best recruiting pitch for the landlocked.

The movies of the 1970s were the apex of surf films, with MacGillivray and Freeman, of Laguna Beach, California, elevating the style. With Bud Browne filming remarkable water shots, their film *Five Summer Stories* turned Hawaiian Gerry Lopez into a celebrity. The slow-motion action of Lopez looking casual while mastering the ferocious tubes of Pipeline had spiritual and mythical appeal.

The surf film as a happening faded with the introduction of videos. Add extreme sports and cable networks such as Fuel TV and surfers didn't need to wait a year to get their heavy-action fix. Still, a few surfing movies struck a chord in the 2000s, particularly *Step Into Liquid* and *Riding Giants,* both of which glamorized such big-wave surfers as Laird Hamilton of Maui, Jeff Clark of Half Moon Bay, and Peter Mel of Santa Cruz, California.

Hollywood encroached on the culture by producing cliché-ridden romantic dramas with beach settings and a hint of surfing. Even Disney gave it a whirl with the animated feature *Lilo and Stitch,* starring an alien and his Hawaiian gal pal who go surfing. Once in a while, though, Hollywood got it right. Amy Heckerling's 1982 spoof, *Fast Times at Ridgemont High,* featured

MY FIVE FAVORITE SURF MOVIES

Blue Crush (2002), John Stockwell
The Endless Summer (1966), Bruce Brown
Five Summer Stories (1972), Greg MacGillivray and Jim Freeman
Going Surfin' (1973), Bud Browne
Riding Giants (2004), Stacy Peralta

TAKING SURF PHOTOS: ADVICE FROM A PRO

Aaron Chang is one of the world's best-known surf photographers. His work has appeared in *Elle*, *Esquire*, *GQ*, *Newsweek*, and *Sports Illustrated* and has been used for many cover shots for surfing publications and in illustrated books. With more than three decades of experience, Chang knows how to get the best shots at your home break or on a surf trip.

Q: I'm not trying to make photography a career, but I want to have some good shots of me and my buddies. What kind of equipment should I use without breaking the bank?

A: The first decision to make in shooting surf photos is whether to shoot digitally or use film. Digital cameras are more complicated in some ways, easier in others. If you are computer literate and you love all things geeky, go digital. If not, shoot film. The biggest single expense will be a long lens (400mm to 600mm). These lenses are necessary to shoot tight action from the beach, like you see in the magazines. The least-expensive entry into surf photography is the water angle. Some waterproof digital point-and-shoot cameras do a good job. The Canon G9 point-and-shoot, with water housing (a waterproof protective covering), is a step up.

Q: What makes a shot great? Is it the lighting, composition, and a zoom lens? Or is there something more?

A: A great surf shot happens by being in the right place at the right time with the right equipment and knowing how to use the equipment. To get something more, you must know what you want to capture and understand how to communicate the moment visually with the viewer.

Q: What do I need to know when shooting from the beach?

A: Always get as close and low as possible to the waves. Get the longest lens you can afford. Remember that with a large digital file, you can always crop the image to make it appear that you have a longer lens than you do. The lower the sun, the better the light will be. Early mornings and late afternoon light make the prettiest pictures.

Q: What do I need to know when shooting from a cliff such as **Steamer Lane** in Santa Cruz, California?

A: Shooting from a cliff or pier is good for a bird's-eye view, but the tighter the better. This is a limited perspective, so be sure not to over-invest your time shooting this angle.

Q: Is it worth getting a water housing for my small digital camera?

A: Absolutely, yes. The water angle is almost always interesting. The cameras that work better for shooting in the water are the ones that allow you to control your shutter speed (action setting on some point-and-shoots). A high shutter speed allows you to freeze the action. Remember that most great water shots are made with either a very wide (fish-eye) lens or a mid-length telephoto lens (80mm to 200mm). The Canon G9 has a 6x optical zoom. Beware of the digital zoom factor, though, since using a digital zoom causes a severe loss of image quality.

Q: Are there safety tips on shooting from the water?

A: Learning to shoot from the water requires an in-depth understanding of surfing and how waves behave. Study this knowledge and develop your swimming skills before you leave the beach. Always use a pair of swim fins that allow you to move through the water with speed and agility. Think of playing water polo as an example of the swimming skill required to shoot water shots. Shoot with your friends first because they will be more forgiving if you interfere with their wave because of bad positioning.

Q: Are there tips on protecting equipment in tropical locales, as well as basic travel safety tips?

A: Most equipment is made fairly well and doesn't require extraordinary care. Keep it dry and clean, do not drop it, and, like a child, never let it out of your sight. Pelican Travel Cases are a must for surf travel. They are waterproof and shock resistant.

Q: What is the most fun part of being a surf photographer?

A: The most fun part is the exploration. You learn to look at—and for—moments of extraordinary beauty. The process alone will lead you down a path that will enhance and elevate your life experience. Throughout the journey, by shooting photos, your efforts will bring positive and joyful creations into the world. To bring joy and inspiration into other peoples lives is unbelievable fun.

Sean Penn as perpetually stoned surfer Jeff Spicoli. With long, blond hair and a surf dialect, Spicoli depicted the stereotypical surfer of the 1980s. In 2002, *Blue Crush* provided a more voyeuristic view of surfing culture. Although the movie ultimately involved a formulaic boy-meets-girl story, the narrative followed a group of young professional surfers living on the beach. The protagonists were independent, strong-willed women who lived to surf. The scenes of their carefree lifestyle rang true. The filmmakers captured a slice of the sport by showing the women driving to a surf spot in Hawaii with music blaring and windows open while singing to their hearts' delight.

COMPETITIVE SURFING

At times it seems as if there are two categories of surfers: the small percentage who thrive on competitive tournaments and the free-spirited personalities who never quite mesh with structured events. However, surfing as a competitive sport dates to ancient times when rival Hawaiian chiefs battled on boards for supremacy. Almost as soon as surfing resurfaced early in the twentieth century, competitions resumed, this time in Hawaii and California. Not much was made of these fledgling tournaments as only a select few surfed at the time. By 1954, though, the seeds of serious competition took root on the west coast of Oahu, where the Makaha International Surf Contest became the de facto world championship.

Within a decade, the sport had changed radically with the mastery of Oahu's classic North Shore spots and the fact that surfing had become an accepted pastime. Image became the priority in the 1960s. To alter surfing's beach-bum perception, sponsors tried to promote a clean-cut persona through organized contests.

The next influential tournament debuted in 1965 in Ventura, California. The Tom Morey Invitational offered all of $1,500 in prize money. Surfing events also became part of the scene on the North Shore and in Australia. It still took another decade for the sport to get serious about organized surfing. Former world champion Fred Hemmings, Jr. and Randy Rarick, both Oahu residents, formed the International Professional Surfers (IPS) in 1976. Although the IPS laid the groundwork for a worldwide tour, it didn't have the financial backing to succeed. The sport got its first major financial break in 1982 when surf-wear giant Ocean Pacific backed former Australian pro Ian Cairns, who organized the **Association of Surfing Professionals (ASP)**. A champion surfer, Cairns has been credited with introducing professionalism into the sport.

THE ASSOCIATION OF SURFING PROFESSIONALS

Ian Cairns started the Association of Surfing Professionals (ASP) in Huntington Beach, California, which made sense with the offices of Ocean Pacific being located in Orange County. It was a daunting task to bring surfing to the level of professionalism found in mainstream sports. For starters, the athletes were unconventional and young. It wasn't easy to shed the sport's party image. Then leaders also had to deal with the backbiting of a competitive industry. It took the group more than a decade of growing pains to develop a solid worldwide tour.

Officials first incorporated the Australian Championship Circuit into the ASP tour. Then they made peace with women professionals to bring them aboard. Since the 1990s, surfing has been a viable, youth-driven sport, if not quite the breakthrough Cairns had hoped. During its early stages, the ASP tour became synonymous with large beach festivals, the kind of sponsors' marketplaces many professional sports now include at events.

The ASP raised the visibility of such notable champions as Kelly Slater, Tom Curren, Lisa Anderson, and Layne Beachley, all crossover stars, which helped to promote surfing beyond its usual demographic boundaries. The ASP contests were held in major media centers so thousands could gather on the beach to watch the final heat on a Sunday afternoon. The formula didn't work because the surf didn't always cooperate by breaking on the weekend, so

ASP officials responded. By the mid-1990s, they began holding contests in some of the world's best spots, even if they weren't particularly spectator friendly. The contests also were scheduled on Mother Nature's timetable, with waiting periods. The move has allowed the world's best to showcase their skills on serious waves, including on the internet with live action. Tour stops now include famous breaks in Australia, Brazil, California, Hawaii, Indonesia, and Tahiti.

In another dramatic move in the early 1990s, surfing went the way of golf by creating a tiered system for men and women. ASP introduced the World Tour (the first division) and the World Qualifying Series (the second division). By having separate tours, ASP could reach more markets and could develop more competitors; today, the organization boasts thousands of members. Eventually, the ASP started sponsoring junior, longboard, and master tournaments also. The tour headquarters moved in 1999 to Queensland, Australia.

Professional surfers can shine when the waves get big.

Despite all the advances, surfing remains a niche sport, struggling to secure long-term sponsorship.

WOMEN'S PRO SURFING

The growth of women's competitive surfing coincided with the general good health of the sport, but it wasn't always that way. In the 1970s, women tried to promote themselves with separate events, such as the Women's International Surfing Association, founded by southern Californians Jericho Poppler and Mary Setterholm. They didn't attract many sponsors because most of their events were held in small waves in California. The organization never got a foothold, but the concept didn't die. Rather, it morphed into the Women's Professional Surfers in the early 1980s. The move paved the way for the women's tour to merge with the ASP.

With women's clothing manufacturers such as Roxy becoming more influential, the opportunities for women surfers increased. Women were able not only to make a living by competing in contests, but they also could be sponsored as free surfers traveling the world to be photographed and videoed—just like the men.

AMATEUR SURFING

About the same time as the original worldwide tour developed, so did contests for high school students. The National Scholastic Surfing Association (NSSA), based in Huntington Beach, California, was begun in 1978 and continues today despite some tumultuous times. Many schools close to the beach have competitive surfing teams, although the sport is not sanctioned by traditional sports governing bodies. As a result, participants aren't awarded varsity letters like football players, swimmers, and golfers are, but the NSSA holds about eighty events a year, including a national championship involving middle school, high school, and college students in California, on the East Coast, and in Hawaii. For those interested in competing, NSSA events provide a good introduction to surfing tournaments. Famous NSSA alumni include Andy and Bruce Irons, Holly Beck, Rob Machado, Bud Llamas, and Alisa Schwarzstein.

HOW CONTESTS WORK

With so many organizations, the contest format has not been standardized. Still, most generally follow a tournament-style system with surfers advancing through heats that last about twenty minutes. A typical contest might have four in a bracket surfing a ten-wave limit. The best two or three rides are totaled with the top two surfers advancing to the next round. According to the ASP judging handbook, "A surfer must perform radical controlled maneuvers in the critical section of a wave with speed, power, and flow to maximize scoring potential."

SURFING AS A CAREER

As enticing as the professional lifestyle may appear, most people don't start out thinking about a surfing career. Many of those who have made it say they took a

Spectators on the bluffs watch the 2007 O'Neill Coldwater Classic surfing contest.

natural trajectory to the professional ranks. Josh Loya, one of California's most versatile professionals, exemplifies the path most youngsters take. He entered his first local amateur contest at age eleven because his friends did. Not interested in organized sports such as Little League, Loya just wanted to surf, but the success he had in the early contests encouraged him to continue competing. He graduated to pro-am events and did well enough to attract the

attention of sponsors. At first, Loya received surfboards and accessories, which was a big deal for a teenager. Then he began working with photographers to get his photo in surf magazines.

Pro surfers develop relationships with photographers to get exposure. Like NASCAR drivers, they plaster their boards with sponsors' decals because grassroots marketing sells to youngsters. A full-page magazine photo of a surfer is worth thousands of

Josh Loya of Santa Cruz, California, was a professional surfer for more than two decades.

dollars in free advertising to companies; surf companies search for the hottest new riders to sign in order to get as many magazine photo spreads as possible.

When Loya was eighteen, he was paid $400 a month to surf. Soon he was making $50,000 a year. He'd spend half the year traveling the world on photo shoots. He stayed with one board builder throughout his twenty-year career, which included being one of the regulars invited to the Mavericks Surf Contest.

When Loya reached his late thirties, though, his primary clothing sponsor dropped him because he had become dispensable in a market targeting thirteen- to twenty-five-year-olds. He planned to ride big waves for as long as he could, but his chances of finding new sponsorship were all but impossible.

Most surfers don't have two-decade careers. After a few years they often join their sponsors in a marketing or executive role. Others open surf shops or get involved in another aspect of the industry.

BEYOND CONTESTS

The contest scene is just one aspect of professional surfing. The sport is fueled by money from clothing manufacturers whose primary interest is getting widespread attention for their brands. Contests are one vehicle for getting that notice, but with an influx of surfing videos, movies, and magazines, the companies also pay master surfers to travel to the world's best breaks for location shoots. This type of sponsorship is called *free riding*. Basically, the surfers are pros without having the constraints of competing in tournaments. One of the biggest

Big-wave surfers ride boards known as guns. These guns were on the beach at Mavericks near Half Moon Bay, California, during a 50-foot day in December 2007.

components of free riding is the revival of big-wave surfing. As the risk factor increases, it seems general interest does too.

BIG-WAVE SURFING

Riding waves bigger than twenty feet is a subset in surfing that few ever master. Some estimates say only 1 percent of surfers regularly practice the art of riding giants. These select few often are mythologized as extreme sportsmen and sportswomen. Overall, surfing is a relatively safe activity until you take off on a potent monster, when the slightest mistake can result in debilitating injury or death.

Greg Noll, the legendary big-wave surfer from the 1950s, rarely thought about the consequences until in 1969 he found himself alone at Makaha Point when the island of Oahu experienced what has been described as a hundred-year swell. Massive waves too big to ride had rolled through Noll's North Shore surfing spots. Sensing the rarity of the moment, the man called "Da Bull" drove to the west side of the island to check Makaha Point, the one break he thought might still be ridable. Noll arrived at the beach as authorities ordered an evacuation. The waves at Makaha were massive but holding. A few intrepid big-wave experts sat far out in the lineup like specks. Noll joined them as a throng gathered on shore to watch the spectacle. As the waves rose to thirty feet or higher, the others paddled to shore, leaving Noll alone in the water. Thirty-two-years-old at the time, he had spent his life challenging big waves, but these were among the biggest he

had seen. Noll has recalled how he had to battle the mental strain about deciding to take off. When a thunderous set rose out of the horizon, Noll picked a wave estimated to be higher than forty feet. He made the drop, but as he straightened the board he fell off the back. No one took photos or video, but witnesses have passed down accounts of the achievement that remains an indelible part of surfing lore.

Noll's journey to big-wave riding began almost twenty years earlier. In the early 1950s he and some buddies had discovered the magical, seven-mile stretch of breaks along the North Shore of Oahu. At the time, few surfers were riding big waves. The cadre of surfers loved the breaks so much they stayed, living out of their jalopies or pitching tents on the lightly inhabited coastline. They survived by spear fishing and eating pineapples and coconuts. The surfers created the beach-bum image on the spot, not that they cared about conventional perceptions.

When giant swells shut down **Sunset Beach** and a handful of other regular spots, the gang discovered the break at Waimea Bay, but no one dared challenge it. Waimea had a mystique that discouraged surfing. A perch overlooking the bay was used by Hawaiian royalty to deliver its babies; a sacred burial site sat nearby. The surfers mostly were spooked by the tale of Dickie Cross and Woody Brown, who got caught in rising surf at Sunset Beach in 1943. They tried to paddle to safety by going through Waimea Bay. Cross, seventeen-years-old, was never found. By

A special breed of surfer is attracted to extra-large swells.

November 1957, though, Noll was entertaining notions of surfing the forebidding wave. On a big but not giant day, Noll and a handful of others, including Pat Curren, Harry Schurch, Del Cannon, Fred Van Dyke, Mickey Muñoz, Bob Bermell, and Mike Stange, met at the bay. Noll, then nineteen-years-old, led an historic paddle into the lineup. The group's conquering of Waimea was received like Sir Edmund Hillary's conquest of Mount Everest four years earlier. Big-wave riding was born. By the next winter more surfers had arrived on the North Shore, this time armed with guns—the specially designed boards.

The big-wave riders were overshadowed by the sport's boom in the 1960s. It would be almost three decades before big-wave riding became an influential part of the sport again. Well-known Hawaiian surfers Mark Foo and Ken Bradshaw paid homage to Noll and his compatriots by making Waimea relevant again, but one unheralded Californian had never stopped riding giants.

Mavericks is one of the best big-wave breaks on the Pacific Coast of North America. It is situated behind Pillar Point. The wave breaks about a half mile beyond the beach, where it is impossible to follow the surfing action.

It took the surfing world fifteen years to catch up to Jeff Clark, though, and the discovery of Mavericks near his hometown of Half Moon Bay, California.

California Discovery

Clark found the big break beyond the cliffs of Pillar Point while in high school. He couldn't get his friends to join him at the break, and few would blame them. The wave at Mavericks comes out of deep water a half mile offshore and breaks over a rocky graveyard. As much as Clark raved about a break as big as Waimea in northern California, few believed him. Half Moon Bay was a quaint, agricultural town known for its October pumpkin festival. In 1990, Clark finally lured two Santa Cruz surfers to Mavericks. That changed everything. The friends told the thriving Santa Cruz surf community about the unfathomable wave. The next winter a crowd arrived, and Mavericks was on the big-wave map just like that. Mavericks offered imposing obstacles that only enhanced its reputation. The paddle to the lineup took forty-five minutes. As a winter's break, the air and water are frosty, the rocky bottom is deep and deadly, and it lies within the Red Triangle, home of white sharks.

In 1994, Mavs entered surfing lore when Foo and Bradshaw arrived to surf a good swell two days before Christmas. A routine outing turned horrific. Foo wiped out on a medium-size wave of about fifteen feet. No one knows what happened, but Foo drowned, probably held down by a surf leash caught on the rocks. Evan Slater,

editor of *Surfing Magazine,* saw Foo's body while heading to shore on a motorized watercraft. He grabbed the lifeless body and took it to the hospital, but it was too late. News of the incident thrust Mavericks into the national spotlight. Throughout the first years of the twenty-first century, the big-wave contest held there attracted fifty thousand spectators, even though the wave is barely visible from shore without binoculars.

Maui Discovery

About the same time that Mavericks gained attention, so did Jaws, a remote North Coast outer reef break on Maui. It was first ridden by windsurfers such as Brett Lickle. Board surfers couldn't paddle into the fast-moving gigantic swells, so they needed help. In 1992, assistance came with the introduction of tow-in surfing by Darrick Doerner, Laird Hamilton, and Buzzy Kerbox. The trio used an inflatable Zodiac to launch into waves near Sunset Beach on Oahu. The concept revolutionized surfing. Personal watercraft, such as Jet Skis, helped boarders ride waves once considered off-limits because the vehicles gave them enough speed to take off on the monsters. The men took their idea to Maui and began their mastery of Jaws. Previous conventions about surfing's boundaries ended.

Tow-in surfing became popular around the globe with surfers challenging bigger and bigger waves. Suddenly surfers were on the prowl to outdo each other for the year's biggest ride. Only a few breaks in the world generate twenty-foot or higher waves under special swell and wind conditions. The best known are Jaws, Mavericks, Todos Santos in Baja California, Cortes Banks far off the coast of San Diego, Ghost Tree in Pebble Beach, California, and Dungeons in South Africa.

Big-wave riders have their own surfing subculture, and they spawned a new realm of competitiveness: the Nissan Xterra XXL Big Surf Awards. The prestigious award recognizes the man and woman photographed on the biggest waves of the year, and big-wave riders now comb the oceans for giant swells, opening new frontiers every year.

The riders are as much surfing stars as the winners of the ASP tour. Hamilton became the sport's biggest breakout star, partially because he understood the art of promotion. Married to model/professional volleyball player Gabrielle Reece, Hamilton has parlayed his fame into commercials, movies, magazine spreads, and documentaries. Through his efforts, as well as those of many others, surfing has found a home among extreme and action sports, and it now rivals conventional sports in appealing to young audiences.

Afterword

Surfing will transport you to a happy place, as Polynesians discovered thousands of years ago. When the early steps seem insurmountable, remember your raison de être: Fun. "It's nice to practice, but it is better just to have fun; if you're not having fun, just go in," says surfing champion Margo Oberg, owner of a famous surfing school in Kauai, Hawaii. All aspects of the learning stages, especially catching your first wave, will leave lasting memories, no matter how far you advance as a surfer.

The first hint of an offshore wind or the crackle of the weather radio announcing a northwesterly headed toward shore is enough to spark a surfer's imagination. And surfing massages the senses: the plaintive cry of a gull or the sudden clap of a cascading wave; the sight of a cylinder of greenish water; the sticky feeling of salty water on the skin. It's enough to draw you back for more.

You may never tow into a jaw dropper at Jaws or sit in the pulsating lineup when Mavericks has awakened from its summer slumber, but that doesn't lessen the thrill of surfing elsewhere. Surfing, you will find, is enjoyable just about any time you hit the beach in search of the elusive perfect wave. It's one of life's little treats, wrapped in the perfumed scent of surf wax, or in shafts of light dancing across the smooth surface of the sea just as the sun begins its daily rise. Even as the sport progresses with technological advancements in board building and gear, the heart of surfing endures as an exercise of free-form expression on nature's undulating stage.

So don't quit after struggling to learn for the first few days. An activity this much fun is worth the effort. It's also worth developing good habits from the start so you can enjoy surfing's beauty after a few months of practice. Surfing may not come quickly, or easily, but it will move you and shape you and call you when it does.

Glossary

360: Skateboard-style aerial turn of a full rotation of the board while suspended midair. The number designates a 360-degree spin. A half rotation of the board is called a 180.

aerial: A daredevil maneuver performed on waves usually six feet and smaller. The tricks originated from skateboarding in empty swimming pools in the late 1970s. The surfer launches his board into the air atop the wave and lands back into the wave's face. The trick was popularized in the 1990s and generated its own following of wave riders.

Association of Surfing Professionals (ASP): Organized by Australian surfer Ian Cairns in 1982 in an effort to form a worldwide governing body. The group has organized a worldwide tour that travels to such locales as Australia, Brazil, California, Fiji, Hawaii, Indonesia, and South Africa. Prize money has increased to a quarter-million dollars for each contest. The schedule also has grown, encompassing two parallel divisions: the World Championship Tour and the World Qualifying Series for men and women.

back-side: The maneuver refers to how one stands on the board; in this case, the rider's back is to the breaking wave. Conventional wisdom says it is easier to control the board while facing the wave because one has better vision down the line. But surfers must learn to ride both ways unless they are switch footers, those who are comfortable standing with either foot forward. Learning to surf back-side is like mastering the backhand in tennis.

Opposite: It's important to find your center of gravity when zipping along a wave.

balsa: A soft, lightweight wood found in Latin America and used as the core for surfboards in the mid-twentieth century before the introduction of polyurethane foam blanks in the mid-1950s. Although many loved their balsa boards, it was cheaper to manufacture foam boards. As a result, the balsa board all but disappeared.

barrel: A hollow section of a wave that creates a fast-moving tunnel. Surfers describe getting "tubed" or "barreled," where they disappear inside the section and then try to pop out.

beach break: One of the major types of breaks. Occurs over a sandbar or sandy bottom. Beach breaks often are dominated by multiple peaks and can be great places to learn to surf if the swell isn't too strong.

blank: The original core material—usually polyurethane foam—that is used to make surfboards. Blanks often are molded into a large chunk that is a basic surfboard shape. A shaper takes the mold and trims and sands it into a more detailed design.

blown-out: A surfing condition describing how onshore winds create choppy waves deemed not worth riding. Wind plays as big a role in good surfing as any natural element. Surfers learn regular wind patterns to know when the conditions likely will be blown-out, resulting in sloppy waves.

board shorts: Swim trunks usually made of lightweight fabrics that dry quickly.

bodyboard: Ubiquitous soft, flexible rectangular boards that are perhaps the most popular ocean toy around. They hark back to the days of surfing's origins when Islanders laid prone while riding waves. The boards got a boost in the 1970s with Tom Morey's super flexible Boogie Board. Bodyboarding is a great introduction into surfing, but it also is a sport in its own right; it has a professional tour organized by the International Bodyboarding Association.

bottom turn: One of the most fundamental maneuvers in surfing, made after dropping down the wave's face. Basically a move to switch directions at the wave's bottom. Can be performed with snaplike precision or more drawn out, depending on wave size and shape. Sets up all other maneuvers on the ride.

breaker: In surfing, synonymous to wave; in essence, a breaking wave with a curl.

breakwater: A seawall of concrete or boulders constructed at harbor mouths or in areas to combat beach erosion. When swells push against breakwaters, they often form well-shaped waves.

bumpy: A condition caused by wind chop where the ocean surface is not smooth. Bumpy waves are not ideal but can be ridden.

caught inside: A situation in which a surfer gets trapped between the shore and fast-moving sets of waves. At breaks with large waves such as Sunset Beach in Hawaii, getting caught inside during a long set can be life threatening because the surfer remains stuck and is sapped of energy after getting smashed over and over again.

chatter: Describes how bumpy the ride is as a board planes across a wave.

choppy: Strong winds result in bumpy waves that are difficult to ride because they lack smoothness to glide across. Surface chop occurs at the first sign of an onshore wind.

clean: Used to describe smooth or glassy waves that haven't been adulterated by onshore wind. A *clean swell* also refers to the size, shape, and direction of the waves because wind is only one factor that impacts conditions.

closeout: When all parts of the wave collapse simultaneously, no shoulder or section remains for planing across the face. Closeout waves usually are found at beach breaks, though they can occur at reefs because of changing tide and groundswell conditions.

cord: Another name for a leash or leg rope. See *surf leash.*

crest: The lip, or top part of the breaking wave. Also called the *curl.*

crumbling wave: Slower-moving wave, with the crest not quite forceful enough to peel over.

curl: The crest or top portion of the wave.

cutback: A maneuver that allows surfers to reverse direction when they get ahead of the breaking curl. Surfers will conduct a cutback to return to the most powerful part of the wave: the curl. Once they cut back, they often will climb and drop on the wave's shoulder. The basic maneuver is called a *roundhouse cutback* and is a classic, smooth turn.

deck: The top of the surfboard where a surfer stands up.

deck grip: A rubber or hardened piece of foam attached to the top of the board for traction.

deepwater break: Because of the natural settings at some surfing locations, swells pass quickly from deep water to shallow, resulting in massive faces.

ding: Any of an assortment of nicks, cuts, cracks, breaks, tears, punctures, or dents in the surfboard's fiberglass coat. Some dings are minor such as shattering a small spot of the deck. Others are deep gouges of the core foam that need immediate attention. Ding repair is one of the most important components of maintaining proper care of surfboards.

drop: See *elevator drop.*

dropping in: Also known as *snaking, cutting off,* or *shoulder hopping,* this is one of the major crimes in the codified world of surfing. The person taking off closest to the curl has the priority, and anyone who drops in front of that surfer has committed a surfing sin. Dropping in is perhaps the biggest reason fights break out in the water.

duck diving: A way to get underneath oncoming waves when paddling to the lineup.

duration: One of the major components in determining wave height and swell strength. It generally is the length of time the wind blows in the same direction over the swell.

dynamic balance: Maintaining stability in an unstable environment through core strength, coordination, and a low center of gravity.

egg: A wide, thin surfboard design for medium to small surfing conditions. It usually has a wide, rounded nose and tail.

elevator drop: A vertical takeoff on a steep, often large, wave.

El Niño: An abnormal warming of the ocean surface in the eastern tropical Pacific. The warmer water conditions can impact weather patterns that can generate Pacific storms, which in turn bring waves to the coast. El Niño conditions also affect climate.

epic: Used to describe a big swell or otherwise great conditions.

expanded polystyrene (EPS): A new core material used to make surfboard blanks. Made with epoxy, a type of plastic resin many prefer to the standard polyester resin that is used to join fiberglass to the polyurethane foam molds. Boards laminated with epoxy are said to be stronger, lighter, and better for the environment.

face: The playful section of the wave just beyond the curl.

feathering: Occurs when the curl is pushed up in offshore wind conditions.

fetch: Generally describes the one-way distance over open water that wind travels to create waves. These waves start off as ripples across the surface and build into bigger waves, eventually joining together to form a groundswell. Fetch, wind speed, and wind duration are the three elements that combine to determine wave height and strength. The longer the fetch, say 1,000 miles, the bigger the waves.

fin: A hard, plastic rudder that is often shaped like a dorsal fin and is attached to the bottom rear of the board. Fins function to allow the surfboard to steer in the direction desired.

The Fish: A board with a spherical nose and split tail first designed in the late 1960s for kneeriding. It was adopted by surfing, becoming the forerunner of the modern-day swallowtail and twin fin designs. The Fish was a very short board used for small waves.

flat: Describes conditions when the surf is not up; lacking waves. Often referred to as a "flat spell" when it persists. Surfers also use the word to describe sections of the wave that are mushy or slow because of changing conditions, such as tide.

foam: Also called *white water*. Part of the broken wave that rushes toward shore in a foamy mush. Foam also is the material used to make surfboard blanks, called foam blanks.

foamies: Surfboards that are made out of soft foam without a hardened fiberglass coat.

foil: A way to measure how the thickness of a board changes from nose to tail. The thickest part of the board usually is in the center. Foil is closely related to the board's rocker.

freefalling: Often occurs during a late takeoff when a surfer and the board are suspended in the air on a particularly steep wave. The vertical fall from space can lead to bad wipeouts.

Gidget: The nickname the famous surfers of Malibu gave to five-foot teenager Kathy Kohner in the mid-1950s. One of them thought she looked like a "girl midget," thus the iconic name Gidget. Also a film of the same name.

glasscoat: The last step in making a surfboard is application of a thin, hard resin, or glasscoat, that gives the board its sheen.

glassy: During windless conditions, the waves are glasslike smooth. Glassy surf is the ultimate for performance because boards plane optimally on a smooth surface. At many surf breaks, the best time to find glassy conditions is in the early morning.

goofy footer: One who stands on a board with the right foot forward. Goofy footers ride front side on left-breaking waves, back side on rights.

green flag: A lifeguard's designation that the surf conditions are safe, usually mild swells without strong rips.

groundswell: Big swells that originate thousands of miles away in the ocean. These swells are vastly different than wind swells.

gun: A specially designed surfboard that is as long as ten feet, with thick rails and a pointy nose. It is made to catch and ride monster waves. The origin of the name comes from "elephant gun," as surfers saw parallels to big-game hunters.

hanging five: See *hanging ten.*

hanging ten: A delicate longboard maneuver that takes supreme balance and also became one of the most popular phrases in surfing vernacular, used by folks who never touched a board. It refers to the act of nose riding in which a surfer places all ten toes over the nose. An ancillary term is *hanging five,* in which the surfer places one foot (five toes) over the edge.

heavy: Describes big, intense waves.

hitting the lip: Advanced maneuver in which the board ricochets off a breaking curl after a surfer performs a bottom turn.

hollow: A concave, curling wave that often is good for tube riding. Hollow refers to any wave that breaks top to bottom forming a cylindrical barrel.

hood: A soft neoprene attachment that protects the head in cold-water environments.

hot coating: One step in the process of building a surfboard. The hot coat is the second layer of resin applied after the initial lamination of the foam blank. This step occurs before the final glasscoat.

impact zone: The intense spot where the curl crashes down on the trough. Getting stuck in the impact zone is the most dangerous place to be while surfing. It also is called the *boneyard* or the *washing machine.*

jack up: Occurs when a wave rises up quickly, usually when a swell passes from deeper water to shallow water. Jacked-up waves are often hollow and challenging.

Jams: Swim trunks for guys that fit loosely around the legs. The term derived from the 1960s. Also known as *baggies.*

Jaws: The Maui surfing spot famous for ushering in the modern big-wave era. The first successfully ridden 35-foot wave occurred at this offshore break, where surfers such as Laird Hamilton perfected the art of tow-in surfing.

Jet Ski: A small, motorized boat, in the category of personalized watercraft (PWC), that is used to zoom around the shore and sometimes up and over waves in a kind of aerial. Jet Skis are often used for tow-in surfing.

jetty: Similar to breakwaters, jetties are built with loose boulders or concrete slabs and are perpendicular to the shoreline. They are constructed to prevent beach erosion or to help form small-boat harbors. Sandbars often build up at jetty tips, forming good waves.

leash: See *surf leash*.

leash plug: A plastic plug inserted into the rear deck of the surfboard. It has a metal bar that is used to attach a leash to the surfboard.

lineup: The area just beyond the break, where surfers sit on their boards and wait for waves or paddle around jockeying for position.

lip: The curl or crest of the wave, often referring to the steep section just as it begins to fold over.

log: A beat-up, heavy, old-fashioned longboard; a *logger* is a surfer who rides one.

longboard: Round-nose boards usually nine feet or longer, they were in vogue until the shortboard revolution of the late 1960s. The longboard revival began in the late 1970s and continues today with new materials and designs making longer boards easier to carry and more functional.

longboarding: Style of surfing with longboards that involves cruising on smaller, slower waves.

Malibu: Perhaps the most iconic surfing break in the world, it is just north of Hollywood and tucked in an enclave where many celebrities live. It has been called the classic California point break and is credited as the place of origin of the surfing culture as we know it.

Mavericks: A famous big-wave break just north of Half Moon Bay, California, that plays host to a winter surf contest attracting 50,000 spectators.

molded boards: A general term used to describe surfboards manufactured by machine mold instead of the traditional manner by hand. The current methods generally use hard plastic shells that are wrapped in layers of epoxy fiberglass.

nose: The pointy or blunt top of the surfboard.

noseguard: Soft, rubber protective device for boards with pointed noses that decreases the chance of injury in a collision and protects the board's tip.

nose riding: A style of riding in which a surfer works his way to the front tip and balances his toes over the front edge.

offshore wind: A wind generated from land that blows toward the ocean. When these gusts hit the face of a wave, they can cause a feathering effect that keeps the breaker from spilling over. In other words, the offshore winds improve the wave's shape for surfing. Surfers usually prefer slightly offshore wind conditions. When they blow too strongly, it can be difficult to paddle into a wave.

off the lip: See *hitting the lip.*

onshore wind: The most common wind found at the beach is generated from the ocean. Onshore winds ruin surfing conditions as waves are "blown-out" or otherwise deemed unworthy.

overhead: A wave, measured from trough to crest, that is greater than the height of the surfer. Measuring waves is a source of constant debate. Some surfers estimate heights from the back; others from the face; the latter results in higher measurements. Some prefer to use themselves as a frame of reference, saying the wave was double overhead, or twice their height while surfing it.

over the falls: Like cascading down a waterfall. Considered the worst type of wipeout because a surfer has little control while caught in the most powerful part of the wave and cast down to the watery hell. The phrase "sucked over the falls" refers to a surfer who is trying to punch through the lip of a big, cresting peak but doesn't quite make it and is pitched backward. The chances of hitting one's head or getting one's wind knocked out are greater when going over the falls.

peak: A wave that comes to a triangular central point, spilling over with nicely rounded shoulders and generally breaking left and right. Beach breaks often are described as "peaky" because waves will rise up at many sandbars in the zone.

pearling: A type of wipeout in which the nose or front of the surfboard dips under the water, abruptly stopping the board. The name derives from pearl diving, and that's what it feels like when the board snags and you go flying off into the abyss.

peel: When a wave breaks perfectly from the curl to down the line, usually at a point break.

peeling waves: Perfect waves to ride, as they rarely have flat spots and are predictable.

Pipeline: The iconic break on the North shore of Oahu that is perhaps the most photogenic wave in the world. It breaks over a shallow coral reef, producing perfect concave tubes.

pitching: When the lip throws out and makes a hollow tube.

pocket: The section of the wave that is steep and usually just ahead of the curl. Small, thin boards made for tube riding often are called *pocket rockets.*

pointbreak: This type of wave generally wraps around a jutting land mass, forming long, smooth lines. Some of the famous pointbreaks are California's Malibu and Rincon, just south of Santa Barbara, and South Africa's Jeffreys Bay.

pop-up: The move one employs to stand up after paddling into a wave, shifting from a prone position and into a crouching stance.

prone: Lying on the belly. It's how you usually ride on a bodyboard and also sometimes how your ride white water into shore.

punch through: Paddling up the wave's face and successfully pushing the board, and body, through the curling lip before it folds over.

quiver: A surfer's collection of different-style surfboards that can be used under varying surf conditions. The quiver generally includes boards of varying lengths, shapes, rocker, fins, and other variables that make each board distinct.

racks: Any devices that hold surfboards on top of cars when transporting them to the beach. Outdoor suppliers Thule and Yakima are big sellers of all types of racks.

rails: The rounded sides of a surfboard from nose to tail on the deck and bottom. Surfers spend a lot of time trying to figure out which kind of rail works best with the waves they ride. Shapers create softer or harder rails depending on preference; they often change the rails' density and hardness throughout the board. In theory, softer, rounded rails make the board easier to handle, whereas harder, sharper rails help with acceleration. Shortboard surfers try to marry the concepts by having harder rails in the tail to generate speed but softer rails at the nose to allow for precision turns.

rash guard: A comfortable Lycra top worn underneath a wetsuit to protect the skin from rubbing against the synthetic rubber. In warm climates, surfers wear rash guards to protect their skin from the sun.

red flag: A lifeguard's designation warning of dangerous surf, inappropriate for swimming. Red flags usually indicate big swells, strong rip currents, and often ideal conditions for big-wave surfers.

Red Triangle: A large coastal zone stretching from Monterey Bay to the Farallon Islands to Tomales Bay in northern California, said to be home to a high number of white sharks. Although shark attacks are rare, the name elicits gruesome images of mauled surfers.

reef break: A wave formed by underwater rock or coral reefs. The waves often have good shape when the swell hits at the right tide. They can produce immense, tubular waves or slower-moving rollers with long, looping shoulders.

reentry: Another term to describe *off the lip*, a reentry occurs when a surfer hits the crown of the wave with the board, which is often pointed toward the sky, and then reverses direction.

reflected wave: Formed when a wave bounces off a jetty and forms a wedge shape that is larger than the original wave.

regular footer: One who stands on a board with the left foot forward. Regular-foot surfers face right-breaking waves, giving them an advantage at many of the famous point breaks.

rhino chaser: A board made for big waves; also called a *gun*, or *elephant gun*.

rips: Also called *rip currents* or *rip tides*, although the strong cross-flow currents have nothing to do with tidal activity. A rip occurs when consistent waves break over a shallow sandbar or reef, carrying water to the beach. That water needs an exit route back to sea, but it can't push its way against the consistent surf. As a result, the outgoing water finds alternate routes, such as deeper water that has fewer waves. By changing direction, it creates a side current as wide as 50 yards. Sometimes the currents create water channels that can be used to paddle to the lineup. Swimmers caught in a rip, though, should swim parallel to shore until exiting the outgoing current. Some also suggest waiting until the fast-moving water pushes the surfer beyond the sandbar before swimming around the rip and then safely to shore. Never try to swim against a rip: It's usually stronger than any person.

river mouth: Where rivers merge with the sea. A fast-moving river can change the ocean bottom by depositing sand and building sandbars that are ideal for surfing. River mouths also often create point breaks by playing a role in changing the landscape. Depending on the location, river mouths often are populated by pinnipeds, such as harbor seals, because of the rich marine life, which attract, in turn, sharks, making river mouths some of the most notorious surfing locations.

rocker: A measurement referring to the curve of a surfboard from the tail to the nose. The board's rocker is important because it determines the flow of water from the bottom of the board. More curvature allows for greater response to turning, especially in the tail section. Less rocker (a flatter bottom) offers greater speed but less maneuverability. Rocker is one of the fundamental characteristics, along with hardness of rails, that shapers consider when building a board. Boards with the same dimensions will respond differently depending on the rocker.

roundhouse cutback: A 180-degree cutback during which a surfer changes direction from the shoulder into the curl.

sandbar: A buildup or rise on the ocean floor, often found at beach breaks where there are river mouths, jetties, and piers.

San Onofre State Beach: California's first state surfing beach and home to the famous surfing club that has had many of the great California pioneers as members. The waves at the popular spot Old Man's are slow rollers that break over a reef ideal for longboarding. It has become one of California's most crowded surfing locations.

section: A self-contained part of a breaking wave that breaks prematurely ahead of the original curl of the wave. The curl of a perfect wave will peel off without any sections. Obviously, most waves aren't perfect, but sections can create great opportunities for maneuvers such as reentries.

set: A group of waves breaking one after the other. When the swell is running strong, it will generate a lot of sets. Some surfers grab the first wave of a set, whereas others show patience and wait to pick off the best wave of the group.

shape: How a wave is described. Many factors such as wind, swell size, tide, and ocean topography factor into how a wave is shaped.

shaper: A person who designs and builds surfboards by hand.

shoaling: A technical term that describes how big waves are formed. Generally, waves approaching the shore hit shallow water and are slowed by the ocean floor, then they are pushed upward, increasing their height.

shore break: Waves that don't break until close to shore, usually not conducive to good surfing because they often fold over simultaneously without forming a tapering shoulder.

shortboard: Boards that came of age in the late 1960s; they are at least three feet shorter and much more streamlined than longboards. Shortboards allow surfers to perform all sorts of tricks on the wave.

shortboarding: Style of surfing that involves using a shortboard to make dramatic turns while riding a wave.

shoulder: The section of the wave beyond the curl, where surfers can carve lines into the wave's face. The shoulder is a more mellow section of the wave than the powerful, peeling lip behind it.

single-fin board: Board that originated in the 1970s. Ranges from 5'5" to 5'7" in varying shapes from nose to tail to rail.

smack the lip: See *off the lip* or *hitting the lip.*

stall: Slowing down the board to let the powerful curl catch up when the surfer has gotten too far ahead of the breaking wave. Surfers stall in order to regain speed and work with the wave.

Steamer Lane: Perhaps the most famous surfing spot in northern California. Located in Santa Cruz at Lighthouse Point. A right-breaking reef wave with outside peaks from the Point, heading south toward the wharf.

steep: Any vertical section of a wave that usually forms a hollow barrel from the lip to the trough.

stick: Slang for a surfboard.

stoked: Slang to express feeling good or happy, especially after a day of surfing.

stringer: The narrow strip of wood found down the center of polyurethane foam blank of a handmade board. The stringer gives the blank strength and is used as a compass by shapers as they cut the template. The stringer helps shapers ensure that both sides of the blank are trimmed symmetrically.

suck out: When a wave suddenly hollows out as it hits a sandbar or reef, usually at low tide. A suck-out wave often breaks hard and greatly increases its size.

Sunset Beach: A major surfing destination on the North Shore of Oahu, located near the Pipeline. Sunset produces big, powerful, right-breaking waves that arrive in the fall and winter months.

surfer's ear: A medical condition also known as exostosis that occurs from exposure to cold water and wind. The inner ear canal is closed off by bone growth, a condition that can lead to hearing loss.

surf leash: The urethane cord that is attached to the back leg and the surfboard. Also known as a *leg rope* or *cord.*

swell: A catchall word for the group of waves that hit the coastline, having been generated from storms thousands of miles away, or from local gusts, which are known as *wind swells.* Also describes a single wave. Surfers designate swells by their direction, such as south, west, or northwest.

tail: The back end of a surfboard. Tail shape influences how a board functions. Surfboards are built with tail variations that involve bluntness, thickness, and shape, such as the V in the swallowtail and the Fish.

takeoff: The moment a surfer has caught the wave while paddling into it, she or he pushes up to "takeoff." This is the motion of a pop-up, where one goes from lying prone into a crouching stance.

template: The basic outline of a surfboard style, often made of wood or fiberboard, that shapers place over a foam blank to trace lines where they will cut. Shapers own a variety of templates, including those for specific nose and tail designs.

Thruster tri-fin: A revolutionary board created by Australian Simon Anderson in 1981. The Thruster was a marriage of the standard single-fin board with the less stable twin-fins. Now some boards have as many as six fins.

Todos Santos: The island off the coast of Ensenada in Baja California that was "discovered" in the early 1980s and is home to big-wave surfing. The waves at Todos Santos blast into the small, remote island with a ferocity seldom seen along the Pacific Coast.

torpedo effect: When a board shoots out from underneath the rider because he or she is sitting or lying too far back.

towboard: These boards are for waves so big one needs to be towed into them by motorized watercraft because paddling is ineffective.

tow-in surfing: The use of personal watercraft to pull surfers into giant surf that would be impossible to paddle into unassisted. Surfers hold onto a long leash as if they were waterskiing while the watercraft propels them forward as the big breaker begins to form. Tow-in surfing has transfigured big-wave riding because it has opened up breaks once considered unapproachable.

trough: Generally, a channel or low point in topography. In surfing, the trough is the low point below a wave's face, the bottom of a wave.

tube: A hollow, powerful section of a cresting wave that breaks like a cylinder from top to bottom. Getting buried in a tube is considered the ultimate experience in surfing, perhaps because of the rarity of barrels big enough to tuck into. Waves create tubes when breaking over shallow reefs, and some rise in the ocean topography.

turning turtle: A basic maneuver to get past the onrushing white water while paddling to a break. It is performed by flipping the surfboard over with any fins facing in the air and holding onto the rails with hands and sometimes feet as the soup passes overhead. Turning turtle is done mostly by longboarders whose cumbersome equipment doesn't allow for duck diving, but beginners need to learn both methods of combating the white water.

twin fin: A surfboard with two fins. The first twin fins were known as the Fish.

Waikiki: A famous Honolulu beach with Diamond Head in the backdrop. It is an ideal spot to learn with slow-breaking rollers that keep their shape for the length of a football field. It's also crowded with tourists and locals. Waikiki is where the original Hawaiian beach boys hung out and created a "beach" culture.

Waimea Bay: One of the original big-wave breaks, with waves up to twenty feet. It has lost some of its mystique as big-wave surfers have discovered bigger, more challenging waves at Mavericks, Jaws, Todos Santos, and Dungeons.

wall: A vertical section of the wave that doesn't taper on the shoulder. When the surf is walled up, conditions are not good for riding waves as it often closes out across the line.

waterman/waterwoman: Someone who embraces the beach life fully, having expertise at surfing, bodysurfing, canoe and board paddling, kayaking, free diving, and spearfishing. This person possesses a wealth of knowledge when it comes to swells, currents, and other aspects of oceanography.

wave: In terms of surfing, the ripple on the ocean's surface that is formed by wind blowing across the water. Basically, these winds transfer their energy onto the water, propelling the mounds of water sometimes thousands of miles toward shore. These swells in the ocean eventually break into what we describe as waves when shoaling from deep water into shallow water that has some kind of undersea topographic landmark, such as a reef or sand.

wax: A gooey bar of paraffin wax mixed with petroleum-based lubricants and chemicals, scents, and dyes that is applied to the deck of the surfboard to give the surfer traction. Different formulas are used for different water temperatures.

The Wedge: A famous bodysurfing break at the south end of the Balboa Peninsula in Newport Beach, California. The rising waves break over a shallow beach, launching bodysurfers and bodyboarders on elevator drops. A number of swimmers have suffered severe injuries while crashing headfirst into the shallow bottom, making the locale one of the most dangerous swimming holes when the swell is running.

wetsuit: A skintight, synthetic rubber suit that protects much of the body against bone-chilling water. Wetsuit accessories include booties, gloves, and hoods.

whitecaps: Strong winds create choppy sea to the point the waves in open oceans crumble into white water before even reaching the lineup. On a blustery day, the ocean will be dotted with whitecaps.

white water: The tumultuous, foamy water created after the curl breaks. The white water dissipates as it reaches the shoreline. Beginners should learn to paddle and stand up while riding relatively calm white water near shore.

wind swell: Whereas almost all waves are created by wind and storms, surfers use the phrase *wind swell,* or *wind waves,* to describe surf generated by localized wind. These waves often are messy and not a great shape for riding.

wipeout: Term used for falling off the board. More colorful expressions such as *over the falls*, *pearling*, and *digging a rail* are used to express the degree of risk involved in the fall.

yellow flag: A lifeguard's designation warning of moderate, and somewhat dangerous, surf. Yellow flags usually indicate conditions best left for expert swimmers and surfers.

Appendix A: Recommended Reading

The following are some of the more interesting books about surfing. Look to these to broaden your knowledge and further your surfing education.

Ahrens, Chris. *The Surfer's Travel Guide: A Handbook to Surf Paradise.* Cardiff-by-the-Sea, England: Chubassco, 1995.

Barrett, Bradley Wayne. *Grannis: Surfing's Golden Age, 1960–1969.* San Clemente, CA: Journal Concepts, Inc., 1998.

Coleman, Stuart Holmes. *Eddie Would Go: The Story of Eddie Aikau, Hawaiian Hero.* Honolulu, HI: MindRaising Press, 2002.

Collier, Ralph S. *Shark Attacks of the Twentieth Century: From the Pacific Coast of North America.* Chatsworth, CA: Scientia Publishing, LLC, 2003.

Collins, Sean. *Surfline's California Surf Guide: Secrets to Finding the Best Waves.* Huntington Beach, CA: Surfline Wavetrak, 2005.

Duane, Daniel. *Caught Inside: A Surfer's Year on the California Coast.* New York: North Point Press, 1996.

Griggs, Ricky. *Big Surf, Deep Dives, and the Islands: My Life in the Ocean.* Honolulu, HI: Editions Limited, 1998.

Guisado, Raul. *The Art of Surfing: A Training Manual for the Developing and Competitive Surfer.* Guilford, CT: Falcon, 2003.

Harrison Clark, Rosie. *Let's Go, Let's Go! The Biography of Lorrin "Whitey" Harrison: California's Legendary Surf Pioneer.* Choteau, MT: Harrison Clark, 1997.

Kampion, Drew. *Stoked: A History of Surf Culture.* Los Angeles: General Publishing Group, 1997.

——. *Greg Noll: The Art of the Surfboard.* Layton, UT: Gibbs Smith, 2007.

Kotler, Steven. *West of Jesus: Surfing, Science and the Origins of Belief.* New York: Bloomsbury, 2006.

London, Jack. *The Cruise of the Snark.* New York: Dover Publications, 2000.

Lueras, Leonard. *Surfing: The Ultimate Pleasure.* Honolulu, HI: Emphasis International/Workman, 1984.

Severson, John, ed. *Great Surfing: Photos, Stories, Essays, Reminiscences, and Poems.* Garden City, NY: Doubleday, 1967.

Twain, Mark. *Roughing It.* New York: American Publishing Company, 1872.

Warshaw, Matt. *The Encyclopedia of Surfing.* Orlando, FL: Harcourt, 2005.

———. *Mavericks: The Story of Big-Wave Surfing.* San Francisco: Chronicle Books, 2000.

Wolfe, Tom. *The Pump House Gang.* New York: Farrar, Straus & Giroux, 1968.

Young, Nat. *Surf Rage.* Sydney, Australia: Nymbodia Press, 2000.

Patient surfers check the waves in the early evening, hoping for a glass-off. (Photo courtesy of Kelly Kenney)

Appendix B: Surfing Resources

Surfing Organizations

Association of Surfing Professionals
Office B, Suite 213, Level 2
Showcase on The Beach, 72-80 Marine Parade
Coolangatta, QLD 4225
Australia
www.aspworldtour.com

Eastern Surfing Association
P.O. Box 625
Virginia Beach, VA 23451
(757) 233-1790
www.surfesa.org

The Groundswell Society
5212 Moonstone Way
Oxnard Shores, CA 93035
glenn@groundswellsociety.org
www.groundswellsociety.org

Opposite: Sleeper sets may catch surfers off guard.

The International Surfing Association
5580 La Jolla Boulevard, PMB #145
La Jolla, CA 92037
www.isasurf.org

National Scholastic Surfing Association
P.O. Box 495
Huntington Beach, CA 92648
(714) 378-0899
www.nssa.org

Surfing America
33157-B Camino Capistrano
San Juan Capistrano, CA 92675
www.surfingamerica.org

Surfing Heritage Foundation
110 Calle Iglesia
San Clemente, CA 92672
www.surfingheritage.org

The Surfrider Foundation
P.O. Box 6010
San Clemente, CA 92674-6010
www.surfrider.org

Museums with Surfing Collections

Bishop Museum
1525 Bernice Street
Honolulu, HI 96817
(808) 847-3511
www.bishopmuseum.org

The British Surfing Museum
Seaside Cottage
69 St. George's Road
Brighton, England BN2 1EF
011-44-7801-522892
www.thesurfingmuseum.com

California Surf Museum
223 North Coast Highway
Oceanside, CA 92054
(760) 721-6876
www.surfmuseum.org

International Surfing Museum
411 Olive Avenue
Huntington Beach, CA 92648
(714) 960-3483
www.surfingmuseum.org

North Shore Surf and Cultural Museum
P.O. Box 754
Waialua, HI 96791
(808) 637-8888
www.captainrick.com/surf_museum.htm

Santa Cruz Surfing Museum
701 West Cliff Drive
Santa Cruz, CA 95060
(831) 420-6289
www.santacruzsurfingmuseum.org

Surf World
Surf City Plaza, Beach Road
Torquay, Victoria
Australia 3228
61-3-5261-4606
www.surfworld.org.au

Surf Forecasting Websites

National Data Buoy Center
1007 Balch Boulevard
Stennis Space Center, MS 39529
http://ndbc.noaa.gov

Storm Surf
PMB 618
80 North Cabrillo Highway, Suite Q
Half Moon Bay, CA 94019
www.stormsurf.com

Surfline.com
300 Pacific Coast Highway
Huntington Beach, CA 92648
www.surfline.com

Swell Info
490 Stamford Drive #308
Newark, DE 19711
www.swellinfo.com

Wave Watch
950 Calle Amanecer, Suite C
San Clemente, CA 92673
www.wavewatch.com

Wet Sand
446 East Main Street
Ventura, CA 93001
www.wetsand.com

Index

About the Author

Elliott Almond, an award-winning journalist and photo enthusiast, caught the surfing bug when still a child living in the Los Angeles beach community of Torrance. He started "hanging five" on skateboards with clay wheels, and graduated to surfing as a teenager living in Orange County, California. He dedicated the next twenty-five years to traveling the coast from Santa Cruz to Mazatlán, Mexico, in search of the perfect wave. A former member of the San Onofre Surfing Club, he helped lifeguard Dan Kenney organize the underground Santa's Chug-a-Lug longboard contest in Newport Beach, California.

Almond wrote a paper on the rise of localism in surfing for a senior-class journalism project at California State University, Fullerton, where he graduated with a bachelor's degree in Communications and a minor in Political Science. Since then he has written stories on the sport of surfing for the *Los Angeles Times, Seattle Times, San Jose Mercury News* and other publications, as well as covering the Olympics and soccer for the *San Jose Mercury News*.

When not chasing guanacos in Patagonia near San Carlos de Bariloche, Argentina, Almond lives in the San Francisco Bay Area where he spends his free time hiking through the verdant redwood forests or at the Central Coast beaches still searching for the elusive perfect wave.

Opposite: The author sits on a mini-mal on a frigid, foggy summer morning at San Francisco's Ocean Beach. (Photo by Tim Harvey)

THE MOUNTAINEERS, founded in 1906, is a nonprofit outdoor activity and conservation club, whose mission is "to explore, study, preserve, and enjoy the natural beauty of the outdoors. . . ." Based in Seattle, Washington, the club is now one of the largest such organizations in the United States, with seven branches throughout Washington State.

The Mountaineers sponsors both classes and year-round outdoor activities in the Pacific Northwest, which include hiking, mountain climbing, ski-touring, snowshoeing, bicycling, camping, kayaking, nature study, sailing, and adventure travel. The club's conservation division supports environmental causes through educational activities, sponsoring legislation, and presenting informational programs.

All club activities are led by skilled, experienced instructors, who are dedicated to promoting safe and responsible enjoyment and preservation of the outdoors.

If you would like to participate in these organized outdoor activities or the club's programs, consider a membership in The Mountaineers. For information and an application, write or call The Mountaineers, Club Headquarters, 7700 Sand Point Way NE, Seattle, WA 98115; 206-521-6001. You can also visit the club's website at www.mountaineers.org or contact The Mountaineers via email at clubmail@mountaineers.org.

The Mountaineers Books, an active, nonprofit publishing program of the club, produces guidebooks, instructional texts, historical works, natural history guides, and works on environmental conservation. All books produced by The Mountaineers Books fulfill the club's mission.

Send or call for our catalog of more than 450 outdoor titles:

The Mountaineers Books
1001 SW Klickitat Way, Suite 201
Seattle, WA 98134
800-553-4453
mbooks@mountaineersbooks.org
www.mountaineersbooks.org

The Mountaineers Books is proud to be a corporate sponsor of the Leave No Trace Center for Outdoor Ethics, whose mission is to promote and inspire responsible outdoor recreation through education, research, and partnerships. The Leave No Trace program is focused specifically on human-powered (nonmotorized) recreation.

Leave No Trace strives to educate visitors about the nature of their recreational impacts, as well as offer techniques to prevent and minimize such impacts. Leave No Trace is best understood as an educational and ethical program, not as a set of rules and regulations.

For more information, visit www.lnt.org, or call 800-332-4100.

Opposite: Dusk brings fond memories of another epic day at the beach. (Photo by Kelly Kenney)

OTHER TITLES YOU MIGHT ENJOY FROM THE MOUNTAINEERS BOOKS

Chasing Waves: A Surfer's Tale of Obsessive Vagabonding
Amy Waeschle
The first travel-adventure book written by a female surfer

The Zen of Oceans and Surfing
Foreword by Gerry Lopez
Explore the peace, tranquility, spirituality, and humor of the world of oceans and surfing.

Don't Get Sunburned
Buck Tilton
For anyone who plays outdoors, this is the most up-to-date guide to protecting your skin.

Conditioning for Outdoor Fitness: Functional Exercise & Nutrition for Every Body, 2nd Edition
David Musnick, M.D., Mark Pierce, A.T.C.
The best-selling book on fitness for outdoor sports

The Road Trip Pilgrim's Guide: Witch-doctors, Magic Tokens, Camping in Golf Courses, and Everything Else You Need to Know to Go on a Pilgrimage
Dan Austin
A vagabond, couch-surfing, road-wise filmmaker-author spins true tales of life with one hand clutching a sleeping bag.

Digital Photography Outdoors: A Field Guide for Travel and Adventure Photographers, 2nd Edition
James Martin
"A great all-in-one reference" —*Digital Photography* magazine

The Mountaineers Books has more than 450 outdoor recreation titles in print.
Receive a free catalog at
www.mountaineersbooks.org